Life Change

S E R I E S

A life-changing encounter
with God's Word from the book of

LUKE

NavPress

Discipleship Inside Out™

NavPress is the publishing ministry of The Navigators, an international Christian organization and leader in personal spiritual development. NavPress is committed to helping people grow spiritually and enjoy lives of meaning and hope through personal and group resources that are biblically rooted, culturally relevant, and highly practical.

For a free catalog go to www.NavPress.com
or call 1.800.366.7788 in the United States or 1.800.839.4769 in Canada.

ISBN 978-0-89109-930-7

Unless otherwise identified, all Scripture quotations in this publicaton are taken from the *HOLY BIBLE: NEW INTERNATIONAL VERSION*® (NIV®). Copyright © 1973, 1978, 1984 by International Bible Society. Used by permission of Zondervan Publishing House. All rights reserved. Other versions used include: the *New American Standard Bible* (NASB), ® The Lockman Foundation 1960, 1962, 1963, 1968, 1971, 1972, 1973, 1975, 1977; the *Revised Standard Version Bible* (RSV), copyright 1946, 1952, 1971, by the Division of Christian Education of the National Council of the Churches of Christ in the USA, used by permission, all rights reserved; and the *King James Version* (KJV).

Printed in the United States of America

12 13 14 15 16 / 15 14 13 12 11

CONTENTS

How to Use This Study   5
    Map of Palestine in Jesus' Time   11
Background—Luke and His Gospel   12
    Outline of the Gospel of Luke   ·   15
    Timeline for Luke's Gospel   18

Galilee

One—Overview (1:1-4)   19
Two—From John to Jesus (1:5–2:52)   29
Three—The Preparation (3:1–4:13)   41
Four—Galilean Ministry Begins (4:14–5:39)   51
Five—Kingdom People (6–7)   61

Journey

Six—From Town to Town (8–9)   75
Seven—With Great Authority (10–11)   89
Eight—On the Alert (12:1–13:17)   101
Nine—Parables and Teachings (13:18–16:18)   113
Ten—The Way to Life (16:19–18:34)   125
Eleven—The Son of David (18:35–19:44)   135

Jerusalem

Twelve—Questions (19:45–21:4)   143
Thirteen—The End Approaches (21:5–22:38)   153
Fourteen—Arrest, Trial, and Death (22:39–23:49)   163
Fifteen—Resurrection and Ascension (23:50–24:53)   173
Sixteen—Looking Back   181

Study Aids   187

ACKNOWLEDGMENTS

The Lifechange series has been produced through the coordinated efforts of a team of Navigator Bible study developers and NavPress editorial staff, along with a nationwide network of fieldtesters.

SERIES EDITOR: KAREN LEE-THORP

Titles in the LIFECHANGE series:

Genesis (#9069X)
Exodus (#92838)
Joshua (#91211)
Ruth & Esther (#90746)
1 Samuel (#92773)
Proverbs (#93486)
Isaiah (#91114)
Matthew (#99964)
Mark (#99107)
Luke (#99301)
John (#92374)
Acts (#91122)
Romans (#90738)
1 Corinthians (95594)
2 Corinthians (#99514)

Galatians (#95624)
Ephesians (#90541)
Philippians (#9072X)
Colossians/Philemon (#9119X)
1 Thessalonians (#99328)
2 Thessalonians (#99921)
1 Timothy (#99530)
2 Timothy (#99956)
Titus (#99115)
Hebrews (#92722)
James (#91203)
1 Peter (#90525)
2 Peter and Jude (#99948)
1, 2, & 3 John (#91149)
Revelation (#92730)

HOW TO USE THIS STUDY

This LIFECHANGE guide to the book of Luke is designed to give students a good overview of the third Gospel. Luke is unique among the synoptics in many ways. Not only does he include many of Jesus' words and deeds that Matthew and Mark omit, but he also emphasizes the work of the Holy Spirit in a way quite unlike the writers of the first two Gospels. And as Luke also is the author of the book of Acts, his Gospel serves as a necessary introduction to the latter book.

Objectives

Although the LIFECHANGE guides vary with the individual books they explore, they share some common goals:

1. To provide you with a firm foundation of understanding and a thirst to return to each book;
2. To teach you by example how to study a book of the Bible without structured guides;
3. To give you all the historical background, word definitions, and explanatory notes you need, so that your only other reference is the Bible;
4. To help you grasp the message of each book as a whole;
5. To teach you how to let God's Word transform you into Christ's image.

Each lesson in this study is designed to take 60 to 90 minutes to complete on your own. The guide is based on the assumption that you are completing one lesson per week, but if time is limited you can do half a lesson per week or whatever amount allows you to be thorough.

Flexibility

LIFECHANGE guides are flexible, allowing you to adjust the quantity and depth of your study to meet your individual needs. The guide offers many optional questions in addition to the regular numbered questions. The optional questions, which appear in the margins of the study pages, include the following:

Optional Application. Nearly all application questions are optional; we hope you will do as many as you can without overcommitting yourself.

For Thought and Discussion. Beginning Bible students should be able to

5

handle these questions, but even advanced students need to think about them. These questions frequently deal with ethical issues and other biblical principles. They often offer cross-references to spark thought, but the references do not contain obvious answers. These questions are good for group discussions.

For Further Study. These questions include: (a) cross-references that shed light on a topic the book discusses, and (b) questions that delve deeper into the passage. You can omit them to shorten a lesson without missing a major point of the passage.

If you are meeting in a group, decide together which optional questions to prepare for each lesson and how much of the lesson you will cover at the next meeting. Normally, the group leader should make this decision, but you might let each member choose his own application questions.

Sometimes there is space in the margins of the study guide to jot answers to optional questions or notes from your discussion. However, you will often want more space for such notes. You can use blank pages between lessons and at the end of the guide for notes, or you can begin a separate Bible study notebook. A separate notebook will give you plenty of room to answer optional questions, record prayer requests and answers to prayer, write notes from discussions, plan applications and record results, and describe experiences in your life that are teaching you spiritual lessons. A notebook like this can be invaluable.

As you grow in your walk with God, you will find the LIFECHANGE guide growing with you—a helpful reference on a topic, a continuing challenge for application, a source of questions for many levels of growth.

Overview and details

The guide begins with an overview of Luke. The key to interpretation is context— what is the whole passage or book about? And the key to context is purpose—what is the author's aim for the whole work? In the first lesson you will lay the foundation for your study by asking yourself, Why did the author (and God) write the book? What did he want to accomplish? What is the book about?

Then over the next fourteen lessons, you will analyze successive passages in detail. You'll interpret particular verses in light of what the whole paragraph is about, and paragraphs in light of the whole passage. You'll consider how each passage contributes to the total message of the book. (Frequently reviewing an outline of the book will enable you to make these connections.) Then, once you understand what the passage says, you'll apply it to your own life.

In lesson 16, you will review what Jesus revealed about His and the disciple's missions in the world and will review the whole Gospel, returning to the big picture to see whether your view of it has changed after closer study. Review will also strengthen your grasp of major issues and give you an idea of how you have grown from your study.

Kinds of questions

Bible study on your own—without a structured guide—follows a progression. First you *observe*: What does the passage say? Then you *interpret*: What does the passage

6

mean? Lastly you *apply*: How does this truth affect my life? The act of wording a question for the guide nearly always makes an interpretation itself, however, so you may want to observe first yourself.

Some of the "how" and "why" questions will take some creative thinking, even prayer, to answer. Some are opinion questions without clear-cut right answers; these will lend themselves to discussions and side studies.

Don't let your study become an exercise of knowledge alone. Treat the passage as God's Word, and stay in dialogue with Him as you study. Pray, "Lord, what do you want me to see here?" "Father, why is this true?" "Lord, how does this apply to my life?"

It is important that you write down your answers. The act of writing clarifies your thinking and helps you remember.

Study aids

A list of reference materials, including a few notes of explanation to help you make good use of them, begins on page 187. This guide is designed to include enough background to let you interpret with just your Bible and the guide. Still, if you want more information on a subject or want to study a book on your own, try the references listed.

Scripture versions

Unless otherwise indicated, the Bible quotations in this guide are from the *New International Version of the Bible*. Other versions cited are the *Revised Standard Version* (RSV), the *New American Standard Bible* (NASB), and the *King James Version* (KJV).

Use any translation you like for study, preferably more than one. A paraphrase, such as *The Living Bible* or *The Message*, is not suitable for study, but it can be helpful for comparison or devotional reading.

Memorizing and meditating

A psalmist wrote, "I have hidden your word in my heart that I might not sin against you" (Psalm 119:11). If you write down a verse or passage that challenges or encourages you, and reflect on it often for a week or more, you will find it beginning to affect your motives and actions. We forget quickly what we read once; we remember what we ponder.

When you find a significant verse or passage, you might copy it onto a card to keep with you. Set aside five minutes during each day to just think about what the passage might mean in your life. Recite it over to yourself, exploring its meaning. Then, return to your passage as often as you can during the day for a brief review. You will soon find it coming to mind spontaneously.

Why group study?

What is the purpose of studying in groups? Two reasons come immediately to mind: *accountability* and *support*. When each member commits in front of the rest to seek growth in an area of life, you can pray with one another, listen jointly for God's guidance, help one another to resist temptation, assure each other that the other's growth matters to you, use the group to practice spiritual principles, and so on. Pray about one another's commitments and needs at most meetings. Spend the first few minutes of each meeting sharing any results from applications prompted by previous lessons. Then discuss new applications toward the end of the meeting. Follow such sharing with prayer for these and other needs.

A group of four to ten people allows the richest discussions, but you can adapt this guide for groups of other sizes. It will suit a wide range of group types, such as home Bible studies, growth groups, youth groups, and workplace studies. Both new and experienced Bible students, new and mature Christians, will benefit from the guide. You can omit or leave for later any questions you find too easy or too hard.

This guide is designed to lead a group through one lesson per week, but feel free to split lessons if you want to discuss them more thoroughly. Or, omit some questions in a lesson if preparation or discussion time is limited. You can always return to this guide for personal study later on. You will be able to discuss only a few questions at length, so choose some for discussion and others for background. Make time at each discussion for members to ask about anything that gave them trouble.

Each member should prepare for a meeting by writing answers for all the background and discussion questions to be covered. If the group decides not to take an hour per week for private preparation, then expect to take at least two meetings per lesson to work through the questions. Application will be very difficult, however, without private thought and prayer.

If you write down each other's applications and prayer requests, you are more likely to remember to pray for them during the week, to ask about them at the next meeting, and to notice answered prayers. You might want to get a notebook for prayer requests and discussion notes.

Notes taken during discussion will help you remember, follow up on ideas, stay on the subject, and clarify a total view of an issue. But don't let note taking keep you from participating. Some groups choose one member at each meeting to take notes. Then someone copies the notes and distributes them at the next meeting. Share these tasks so that everyone will feel included and no one will feel burdened. Some groups have someone take notes on a large pad of paper or erasable marker board (preformed shower wallboard works well), so that everyone can see what has been recorded.

Structuring your group time

The following suggests one possible way to structure your discussions. You should adapt these suggestions in whatever way best suits your group.

Worship. Some groups like to begin with prayer and/or singing. Some pray only briefly for God's guidance at the beginning, but leave extended prayer until after the study.

Warm up. Profitable studies early on lay a good foundation for honest sharing

8

of ideas, for getting comfortable with each other, and for encouraging a sense of common purpose. One way to establish common ground is to talk about what each group member hopes to get out of your study and out of any prayer, singing, outreach, or anything else you might do together. You might also discuss what you hope to give to the group. If you have someone write down each member's hopes and expectations, then you can look back at these goals later to see if they are being met. You can then plan more time for prayer or decide to move more deliberately through the study.

Take some time at the outset to talk about goals. Some groups use one session to hand out study guides, introduce the study, examine pages 5-10 in this section, and discuss goals.

First impressions. You may find it helpful to discuss each member's first impressions as you progress through the study. What was most helpful? Did anything startle you? What questions do you have? What overall impression did you gain from the session?

To focus your discussion, you might ask each group member to choose one scene or teaching that was especially meaningful to him or her, and explain why. This open sharing often helps members to get to know one another better.

Study. Follow the study guidelines in whatever manner best helps you to grasp the meaning of the biblical text. It should be your overarching goal to gain a thorough understanding of the passage under review.

Application. The last step of Bible study is asking yourself, "What difference should this passage make to my life? How should it make me want to think or act?" Application will require time, thought, prayer, and perhaps discussion with someone else.

At times, you may find it most productive to concentrate on one specific application, giving it careful thought and prayer. At other times you may want to list many implications a passage of Scripture has for your life, and then choose one to focus on for prayer and action. Use whatever method helps you to grow more obedient to God's Word.

Some possible applications for a passage: "I need to ask God for the ability and discipline to obey by His Spirit." "I need to stop . . . " "I need to ask the Holy Spirit to help me . . ." "I believe I should . . ."

As you develop applications, remember that we must cooperate with God if we are to grow spiritually; both we and God have a part to play (Philippians 2:12-13). Effective applications must be saturated with prayer for guidance, ability, forgiveness, discipline, encouragement, etc.

If application is unfamiliar to some group members, choose a sample paragraph from the Gospel and discuss possible ways of applying it. Try to state specifically how the passage is relevant to you and how you might act in light of it. Think of responses that you might actually make, not merely ideal responses. Don't neglect prayer for ability, courage, discipline, and guidance to carry out the response you have identified!

Give the group a chance to voice any questions about the passages under review or historical/cultural references that may puzzle them. You may decide to postpone answering some questions until you have access to appropriate information, but do try to keep the group's questions in mind.

Wrap-up. The wrap-up is a time to bring the discussion to a focused end and to make any announcements about the next lesson or meeting. Most of the lessons in this study cover more than one chapter of the Gospel; your group may decide to tackle some of these lessons in more than one session. Make sure you decide ahead of time how much of each lesson you plan to study at your next session.

Worship. Praise God for His wisdom in giving us the teachings, principles, inspiration and encouragement found in the Gospel of Luke. Praise Him for what He reveals about Himself in this book and ask Him to teach you to know, love, and obey Him throughout your study of Luke.

Beyond these suggestions, page 190 lists some good sources of counsel for leading group studies.

Map of Palestine in Jesus' Time

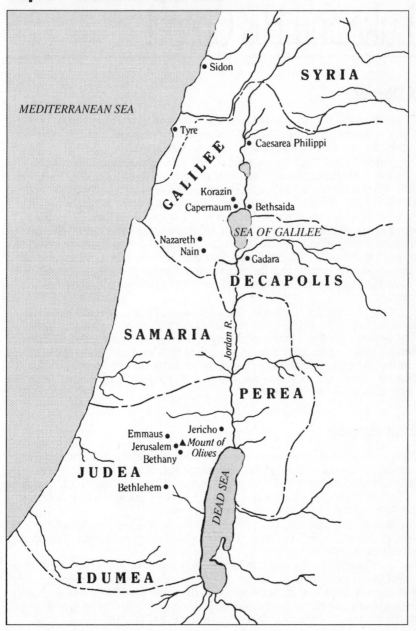

MEDITERRANEAN SEA

• Sidon

SYRIA

• Tyre

• Caesarea Philippi

GALILEE

Korazin
Capernaum • • Bethsaida

SEA OF GALILEE

Nazareth •
Nain •

• Gadara

DECAPOLIS

SAMARIA

Jordan R.

PEREA

Emmaus •   Jericho •
Jerusalem • ▲ Mount of
Bethany •   Olives

JUDEA

Bethlehem •

DEAD SEA

IDUMEA

Luke and His Gospel

A Gospel

Gospel is an Old English word that means "good news." It is a translation of the Greek word *euangelion* (*eu-*, "good" and *angelion,* "message"), and also gives us words like "evangelist" and is related to words like "angel."

When the first Christians wanted to record the "good news" about the Man who was God, none of the familiar forms of literature seemed suitable. The Christians didn't write the kinds of autobiographies or sacred texts that were common in Greek, Roman, or Jewish culture. Instead, they created a new form: the Gospel.

The Gospels were composed of scenes and sayings from Jesus' life remembered by His disciples and passed on, probably word for word. Oriental disciples learned by committing their master's words and actions to memory for imitation. As Leon Morris notes, "Rabbis used to cast their teaching into forms suitable for memorization and insist that their pupils learn it by heart."[1] The apostles faithfully recalled both individual statements and the overall progress of Jesus' time with them.

Luke said that by the time he wrote his Gospel, "Many have undertaken to draw up an account of the things that have been fulfilled among us . . ." (Luke 1:1). Apparently, other Christians had begun to record what the apostles remembered of Jesus' words and deeds. The Gospel of Mark may have been among several written sources Luke had available when he wrote his "orderly account" (Luke 1:3) of Jesus' ministry. Luke was also able to speak to people who had known Jesus (see "Physician and writer" on page 13).

Four Gospels

Many collections of Jesus' words and deeds were composed in the first century after His death, but God uniquely inspired four men to write the Gospels that would bear His authority. Why four? We can speculate, or we can simply be glad for all four masterful portraits that reveal our Lord in different lights. As J. Sidlow Baxter asks, which of the four could we do without?[2]

It is striking how coherent a picture of a single man and a single set of events emerges from four such different points of view. Observe the distinct interests and emphases in these examples:

1. To Matthew, who writes for Jewish Christians, Jesus is above all the King of David's line promised in the Hebrew Scriptures and the Teacher who brings a new revelation of God's Law. Matthew weaves fulfillments of Old Testament prophecies around five discourses about the Law and the Kingdom. Mark pens a short Gospel in quick scenes that drive toward the cross, revealing Christ more in works of

power and service than in words of wisdom. John records a few miraculous signs and several long discourses to spark faith in God the Son. And Luke crafts his account of the Son of Man, the Savior of the world, to be meticulously accurate and also captivating for a cultured Greek audience.

2. John begins with Jesus' pre-existence as God, and Mark starts with Jesus' baptism as an adult. Neither tells of Jesus' birth or lineage. Matthew opens with a genealogy that traces from Abraham (the father of the Israelite covenant), to David (the head of the Jewish royal line) and finally to Joseph (Jesus' legal father in Jewish eyes, though not His natural one). Matthew's birth account focuses on kingship and prophecy, while Luke narrates the birth with warm, human touches. He also traces Jesus back to Adam—the father of Jew and Gentile alike—and then to God. Matthew's Jewish-minded nativity focuses on men, but Luke delights in pregnant women and old widows.

3. John highlights Jesus' ministry in Jerusalem. Matthew and Mark describe mainly His Galilean ministry and His last week in Jerusalem. But Luke includes ten long chapters in which Jesus journeys toward Jerusalem, training His disciples. We call Matthew, Mark, and Luke the *synoptic* (one view) Gospels because they have much more material in common than any of them has with John. Yet Luke's description of the journey to Jerusalem includes at least thirty incidents, parables, and sayings that Matthew and Mark omit.

As you study Luke's Gospel, we will point out more features that mark its unique contribution to Scripture.

Physician and writer

Luke was Paul's "beloved physician" (Colossians 4:14). He traveled with Paul on the apostle's second missionary journey. When Paul reached Philippi, Luke probably remained there (Acts 16:10-17) and some years later left Philippi with Paul (Acts 20:6-38). Luke went with Paul to Palestine (Acts 21:1-18) and stayed for some time with Philip the evangelist in Caesarea. When Paul was arrested in Jerusalem and sent as a prisoner to Rome, Luke accompanied him (Acts 27:1–28:16). These travels gave Luke opportunities to meet many of Jesus' original disciples and eyewitnesses to His life, and also to absorb Paul's understanding of the Savior of all people. Because Luke recorded several events in Mary's life that the other Gospels do not include, many people suspect that Luke may have interviewed her about her Son.

Although Luke was present at some of the events he recorded in the Acts of the Apostles, he was not an eyewitness of anything in his Gospel (Luke 1:2-3). We believe he was born a Gentile, but he may have become a Jew before he heard of Christ. Luke was steeped in the urban, Gentile, Greek-speaking culture of the Roman Empire; the prologue to his Gospel shows that he could write literary Greek when he so chose. Also, Luke was well versed in the *Septuagint*, the Greek translation of the Old Testament used by Jews all over the empire.

We can sometimes detect signs of Luke's training as a physician in the details he chose to include. When recounting healing miracles, for example, he used technical Greek medical words to describe the ailment (5:12, 14:2), while Matthew and Mark used laymen's terms. Luke included sayings in which Jesus compared Him-

13

self to a physician (4:23, 5:31) that the other Gospels omitted, but in 8:43 he omitted the report that the bleeding woman spent all her money on doctors to no avail (Mark 5:26). Luke was especially fond of the words *salvation* and *saved*, which in Greek also meant *healing* and *healed* (1:71; 2:30; 7:50; 8:36,48,50; 9:1-2,42; 17:19; 19:9-10; 23:35-39). Finally, the physician used his skills of minute observation and interview to give us precise accounts of many events.

When Luke wrote

Suggested dates for Luke's Gospel vary. Leon Morris favors the early 60s AD, since Acts ends abruptly in AD 62 and nothing in either book demands a later date.[3] I. Howard Marshall leans toward a date shortly before or after AD 70, noting Luke's interest in Jesus' prophecies of the destruction of Jerusalem, fulfilled in AD 70.[4] Dates as late as AD 110 have been suggested.

Theophilus

Luke's Gospel is the longest book in the New Testament. At that time, books were handwritten on scrolls of papyrus reed, and a papyrus scroll could scarcely have been made longer without falling apart. But despite its length, Luke's Gospel must have intrigued its literary Greek audience.

The book is addressed to "Theophilus" (1:3), which means "lover of God." Luke may have made up a name to symbolize all those who would come to his book to learn about Jesus. Yet it was common in Luke's day to write for and dedicate a book to a wealthy patron, who helped to pay for publishing the manuscript. Theophilus was a common Greek name, and this man may have been an educated Gentile aristocrat, either a new convert or an interested pagan. Unlike Matthew, Luke made a point of explaining Jewish practice and events so as to help a Gentile understand them.[5]

1. Leon Morris, *The Gospel According to Saint Luke* (Grand Rapids, Mich.: William B. Eerdmans Publishing Company, 1974), page 30.
2. J. Sidlow Baxter, *Explore the Book*, volume 5 (Grand Rapids, Mich.: Zondervan Corporation, 1966), pages 117-125, 229.
3. Morris, pages 22-26.
4. I. Howard Marshall, *The Gospel of Luke* (Grand Rapids, Mich.: William B. Eerdmans Publishing Company, 1978), pages 34-35.
5. Marshall, page 43; Morris, pages 66-67.

Outline of the Gospel of Luke

A. Prologue (1:1-4)
B. The infancy stories (1:5–2:52)
    1. John's birth foretold (1:5-25)
    2. Jesus' birth foretold (1:26-38)
    3. Mary visits Elizabeth (1:39-56)
    4. John's birth (1:57-80)
    5. Jesus' birth (2:1-20)
    6. Jesus presented at the Temple (2:21-40)
    7. Jesus at twelve (2:41-52)
C. From John the Baptist to Jesus (3:1–4:13)
    1. The message of John (3:1-20)
    2. The baptism of Jesus (3:21-22)
    3. The genealogy of Jesus (3:23-37)
    4. The temptations of Jesus (4:1-13)
D. Jesus' ministry in Galilee (4:14–9:50)
    1. Jesus at Nazareth (4:14-30)
    2. Healings in Capernaum (4:31-44)
    3. The first disciples called (5:1-11)
    4. A leper cleansed (5:12-16)
    5. A paralytic healed (5:17-26)
    6. Jesus and sinners (5:27-32)
    7. Fasting (5:33-39)
    8. The Sabbath (6:1-11)
    9. The choice of the Twelve (6:12-16)
    10. The sermon on the plain (6:17-49)
    11. A centurion's servant healed (7:1-10)
    12. A woman's son resurrected (7:11-17)
    13. Jesus answers John the Baptist (7:18-23)
    14. Jesus discusses John the Baptist (7:24-35)
    15. A sinful woman anoints Jesus (7:36-50)
    16. Women who helped Jesus (8:1-3)
    17. The parable of the four soils (8:4-15)
    18. The parable of the lamp (8:16-18)
    19. Jesus' true family (8:19-21)
    20. A storm stilled (8:22-25)
    21. The Gerasene demoniac (8:26-39)
    22. A girl raised, a woman healed (8:40-56)
    23. The Twelve sent (9:1-6)
    24. Herod's question (9:7-9)
    25. Five thousand fed (9:10-17)
    26. Who is Jesus? (9:18-27)
    27. The Transfiguration (9:28-36)
    28. A deliverance and a perplexing promise (9:37-45)
    29. An argument (9:46-50)

E. Travel toward Jerusalem (9:51–19:44)
  1. Samaritan opposition (9:51-56)
  2. The cost of discipleship (9:57-62)
  3. The mission of the seventy-two (10:1-20)
  4. Thanksgiving (10:21-24)
  5. The lawyer's question (10:25-28)
  6. The good Samaritan (10:29-37)
  7. Serving Jesus (10:38-42)
  8. Prayer (11:1-13)
  9. Jesus and Beelzebub (11:14-26)
  10. True blessedness (11:27-28)
  11. The sign of Jonah (11:29-32)
  12. The lamp of the body (11:33-36)
  13. Six woes (11:37-54)
  14. Fearless confession (12:1-12)
  15. The rich fool (12:13-21)
  16. Anxiety (12:22-34)
  17. Readiness (12:35-48)
  18. Division (12:49-53)
  19. Discernment (12:54-59)
  20. Repentance (13:1-9)
  21. A Sabbath cure (13:10-17)
  22. Kingdom parables—mustard seed and yeast (13:18-21)
  23. The narrow door (13:22-30)
  24. Prophets die in Jerusalem (13:31-35)
  25. Another Sabbath healing (14:1-6)
  26. Banquet manners (14:7-14)
  27. The parable of the great banquet (14:15-24)
  28. The cost of discipleship (14:25-35)
  29. Parables of the sheep, coin, and son (15:1-32)
  30. Parable of the shrewd manager (16:1-9)
  31. Faithful stewardship (16:10-13)
  32. The Pharisees reproved (16:14-18)
  33. The rich man and Lazarus (16:19-31)
  34. Sin and faith (17:1-10)
  35. The grateful Samaritan (17:11-19)
  36. The coming of the Kingdom (17:20-37)
  37. The unjust judge (18:1-8)
  38. The Pharisee and the tax collector (18:9-14)
  39. Jesus and children (18:15-17)
  40. The rich ruler (18:18-30)
  41. The third prediction (18:31-34)
  42. A blind man healed (18:35-43)
  43. Zacchaeus the tax collector (19:1-10)
  44. The parable of the ten minas (19:11-27)
  45. The triumphal entry (19:28-40)
  46. Lament over Jerusalem (19:41-44)
F. Jesus' ministry in Jerusalem (19:45–21:38)

1. The cleansing of the Temple (19:45-48)
2. A question of authority (20:1-8)
3. The parable of the wicked tenants (20:9-19)
4. A question of taxes (20:20-26)
5. A question about resurrection (20:27-40)
6. Jesus' question (20:41-44)
7. The teachers criticized (20:45-47)
8. The widow's offering (21:1-4)
9. Signs of the end (21:5-38)
G. The Passion and Resurrection (22:1–24:53)
1. The Last Supper (22:1-38)
2. Jesus prays in Gethsemane (22:39-46)
3. Jesus arrested (22:47-53)
4. Peter's denials (22:54-62)
5. Before the Sanhedrin (22:63-71)
6. Before Pilate and Herod (23:1-25)
7. Crucifixion (23:26-43)
8. Death (23:44-49)
9. Burial (23:50-56)
10. Resurrection (24:1-12)
11. The walk to Emmaus (24:13-35)
12. The appearance to the disciples (24:36-49)
13. The Ascension (24:50-53)

TIMELINE FOR LUKE'S GOSPEL

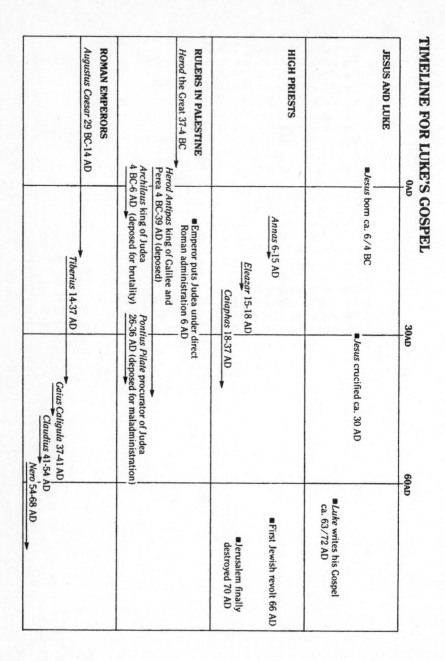

	0AD	30AD	60AD
JESUS AND LUKE	■ *Jesus born ca. 6/4 BC*	■ *Jesus crucified ca. 30 AD*	■ *Luke* writes his Gospel ca. 63/72 AD
HIGH PRIESTS	*Annas 6-15 AD* / *Eleazar 15-18 AD* / *Caiaphas 18-37 AD*		■ First Jewish revolt 66 AD ■ Jerusalem finally destroyed 70 AD
RULERS IN PALESTINE	*Herod the Great 37-4 BC* ■ Emperor puts Judea under direct Roman administration 6 AD / *Herod Antipas king of Galilee and Perea 4 BC-39 AD (deposed)* / *Archilaus king of Judea 4 BC-6 AD (deposed for brutality)* / *Pontius Pilate procurator of Judea 26-36 AD (deposed for maladministration)*		
ROMAN EMPERORS	*Augustus Caesar 29 BC-14 AD* / *Tiberius 14-37 AD*	*Gaius Caligula 37-41 AD* / *Claudius 41-54 AD* / *Nero 54-68 AD*	

18

Luke 1:1-4

Overview

The best way to introduce yourself to Luke's Gospel is to read it through, in one sitting if possible. It should take you about two hours if you read quickly for an overall impression. If your Bible includes subtitles for passages, use them as clues to the story's movement.

As you read, jot down answers to questions 1-6. Questions 7 and on relate to particular sections of Luke's Gospel.

For Further Study: Look for examples of the following in Jesus' teaching and actions:
- Ordinary people
- Medical interest
- Personal details (like age)
- Signs of emotion

First impressions

1. What are your first impressions of Luke's book? What is it about? What overall impression does it give you of Jesus? If you had to pick a single term to describe Luke's Gospel, what would it be?

_____

_____

_____

_____

_____

_____

19

2. Repetition is a clue to the ideas an author wants to stress. What key words or phrases does Luke (or Jesus) use over and over?

_____

_____

_____

_____

_____

_____

3. Look for at least one example of each of the following of Luke's (and Jesus') interests.

a. Poverty

in Jesus' personal life _____

_____

_____

in Jesus' teaching _____

_____

_____

_____

in people Jesus encountered _____

_____

_____

_____

b. Women

people Jesus encountered _____

_____

_____

in Jesus' teaching _____

_____

_____

_____

c. Prayer

in Jesus' personal life _____

_____

_____

_____

in His teaching _____

_____

_____

_____

in others' lives _____

_____

_____

_____

d. The Holy Spirit

in Jesus' personal life _____

_____

_____

_____

in His teaching _____

_____

_____

_____

in others' lives _____

_____

_____

e. Salvation for the whole world

in Jesus' teaching _____

_____

_____

_____

in words about Jesus _____

_____

_____

_____

in Jesus' actions _____

_____

_____

_____

4. The practice of outlining often helps tremendously
in obtaining a good grasp on the flow and general
contents of a book. Fill in the following "skeleton"
with your own reference numbers (chapter and
verse numbers) for each section, as well as appropriate titles. (There may be more blank lines provided than what you decide you need.) A detailed
outline appears on pages 15-17.

Passage   **Title**
1:1-4   Prologue
1:5–4:13   Prelude to ministry

_____

_____

_____

Passage   **Title**

_____

_____

_____

Passage   **Title**
4:14–9:50   Ministry in Galilee

_____

_____

_____

_____

_____

_____

_____

_____

_____

Passage   **Title**
9:51–19:44   Travel toward Jerusalem

_____

_____

_____

_____

_____

_____

Passage   **Title**

_____

_____

_____

_____

Passage   **Title**
19:45–21:38   Ministry in Jerusalem

_____

_____

_____

_____

Passage   **Title**
22:1–24:53   Passion and Resurrection

_____

_____

_____

_____

_____

_____

5. Note here any incidents, teachings, topics, or
   impressions of Jesus in Luke's Gospel that you
   want to think about this week.

_____

_____

_____

_____

_____

_____

_____

_____

6. In your first reading of Luke's Gospel or in the background on pages 12-14, you may have encountered some concepts you'd like clarified or questions you'd like answered. While your thoughts are still fresh, jot down your questions here. You can look for answers as you study further.

_____

_____

_____

_____

_____

_____

_____

Prologue

In classical Greek style, Luke begins his work with a formal dedication to his patron (the man who is probably helping to pay for publishing the book). The dedication offers several clues to Luke's intent in writing this book.

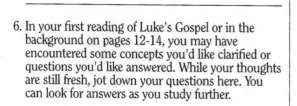

Study Skill—Themes and Purposes
Before you study a book in detail, it is helpful to make some tentative conclusions about the book's themes and purposes. A *theme* is a main topic that recurs through the book, such as "salvation." A *purpose* is a reason the author wrote, such as "to teach Gentile readers about salvation."
(continued on page 26)

For Thought and Discussion: What is your own purpose for studying Luke's Gospel? How does it compare with 1:4?

(continued from page 25)
One reading of Luke's Gospel may not give you a firm sense of his main themes and purposes, but by now you probably are at least beginning to have some ideas about what they may be. Don't be hesitant to express those ideas; remember, they're tentative!

7. Read 1:1-4 slowly several times, preferably in several translations. What subject does Luke say he is writing about? (Think about what "the things that have been fulfilled [NASB: "accomplished"] among us" are.)

_____

_____

_____

_____

_____

_____

_____

8. What does *Luke* identify as his purpose for writing his Gospel (1:3-4)?

_____

_____

_____

_____

_____

_____

9. From what you know of Luke's Gospel so far, try to summarize in your own words what *you* think is the purpose of this book.

_____

_____

_____

_____

_____

_____

10. What issues in your own life already have been raised by your quick reading of Luke? How are you planning to deal with these issues in the coming week?

_____

_____

_____

_____

_____

_____

_____

Study Skill—Outlining the Purpose
An ordinary outline of Luke's Gospel such as the one on pages 15-17 can help you find particular passages, but it tells you little of how the parts fit into Luke's overall message. One way to recall Luke's message at a glance is to outline the way each passage unfolds that message.

For instance, Luke's purpose is to set forth the good news about Jesus in an orderly manner, so that the reader can respond to that news. A broad outline of the book that takes account of this purpose might begin like this:

(continued on page 28)

(continued from page 27)

1:1-4 Prologue: Luke states the purpose of his book.

1:5–2:52 Infancy: The Savior and His herald are born miraculously into our world, announced by angels and prophets. The Son of God becomes a Son of Adam.

3:1–4:13 The Savior's herald introduces the good news about repentance and forgiveness. The Savior is declared Son of God and undergoes baptism and temptation as Son of Man—all in preparation to begin His mission.

Get a sheet of paper and begin your own outline of Luke's Gospel that reflects his purpose and themes. You can make up your own summaries for 1:1–4:13 or copy these and begin your own outline with 4:14-44. Try to add a new entry as you complete each lesson.

Luke 1:5–2:52

From John to Jesus

In lesson 1 you thought about the purpose of Luke's
Gospel. One simple summary of that purpose is: "To
explain the good news about Jesus." For the rest of this
study, we will focus on this purpose. We will look for
the *content* of the good news and the *response* Luke
urges us to make to it. The content is Jesus—His identity, character, mission, and message.

For this lesson, read through all of 1:5–2:52 first.
You would benefit from reading it in several different
translations. Ask God to enlighten your mind to understand and soften your heart to respond.

Luke's style changes in 1:5. The prologue (1:1-4)
is in literary Greek, but the infancy stories use a
Hebrew style of speaking.[1] Many of the scenes and customs of Jewish Palestine would have been as foreign to
Luke's Greek-Roman audience as they are to us. The
ethnic style and exotic setting must have made this tale
of angels and miracle births seem even more improb-
able to a sophisticated man like Theophilus. Perhaps
Luke wanted his patron to face squarely the extraordinary way God had chosen to intervene in history.[2]

As you read 1:5–2:52, do the following:

1. Look for important words. Find in a dictionary
   or note in the study guide's margins any words
   you do not understand.
2. Get a sense of what the passage is about.

When you have read 1:5–2:52 once, then go back
and work on the questions below. Use the margins and

29

Verse 17 recalls Malachi 3:1, 4:5-6.

a. What do you think "to turn the hearts of the fathers to their children" means?

b. Why do you think turning fathers' hearts to their children is part of preparing the people for the Lord to come?

Optional Application:

a. Have you ever responded to God's promises as Zechariah did (1:18)? What tempts you to do this, and how can you overcome this temptation?

b. Contrast Zechariah in Luke 1:11-20 with Abraham in Genesis 15:1-6, 17:15-21.

For Thought and Discussion:

a. Compare Mary's response in 1:34 to Zechariah's in 1:18. Why did Mary receive no rebuke?

b. How can you cultivate Mary's attitude?

any other blank space to jot thoughts on the optional questions. If an idea for personal application strikes you, turn to page 38 and write your idea under question 14, so that you won't forget it.

John's birth foretold (1:5-25)

Herod (1:5). Herod the Great ruled Judea from 40³ to 4 BC. The events of chapters 1 and 2 took place near the end of his reign.

Your prayer has been heard (1:13). It was customary for the priest who offered the evening sacrifice to pray for the deliverance of Israel from oppression. Since Zechariah had won the once-in-a-lifetime chance to offer the evening incense, he was probably thinking of his priestly office rather than his personal desires.[4]

Wine (1:15). A man could vow to abstain from alcoholic drinks and from cutting his hair as a special act of dedication to the Lord. Such a man was called a "Nazirite" (Numbers 6:1-21). Samson (Judges 13:4-7) and Samuel (1 Samuel 1:11) were dedicated as Nazirites from birth.

1. What do you learn from 1:5-25 about each of the following:

John the Baptist's mission (1:15-17)

_____

_____

_____

_____

_____

How people should respond (1:14-20)

_____

_____

_____

_____

_____

For Further Study:
Notice the repeated
word "joy" in
1:14,44,47,58; 2:10.
What is Luke's point?

Disgrace (1:25). Barrenness was regarded as divine disfavor. Elizabeth's experience repeated Sarah's (Genesis 16–17,21) and Hannah's (1 Samuel 1–2).

Optional Application:
Respond to God's deeds
of salvation for you as
Mary and Elizabeth did.

Jesus' birth foretold (1:26-38)

Pledged (1:27). Betrothal was a binding contract breakable only by divorce.

His father David (1:32). God had promised that a descendant of King David would inherit his throne and reign permanently over Israel (2 Samuel 7:13,16; Isaiah 9:6-7). The Jews called this descendant the *Messiah* (Greek: *Christ*), which means "Anointed One."

2. Gabriel said two things about Jesus' identity (1:32-33). Who was Jesus going to be?

_____

_____

_____

_____

Mary visits Elizabeth (1:39-56)

The hymn in 1:46-55 is known as the Magnificat because its first word in Latin is *Magnificat,* "glorifies." Luke includes three other hymns in 1:5–2:52.

Some people think Mary was praising God for what He did in Old Testament times; others think she was prophesying what God was beginning to do through Jesus. Old Testament prophets often spoke of the future in the past tense (Isaiah 53) to show the certainty of the prediction.

31

3. Mary calls God "my Savior" in 1:47. How does she portray God as Savior in 1:48-55?

_____

_____

_____

_____

_____

4. What does 1:39-56 reveal about Jesus' identity and mission (1:43,51-55)?

_____

_____

_____

_____

5. How do Mary and Elizabeth respond to this revelation?

_____

_____

_____

_____

John's birth (1:57-80)

Salvation (1:69). This is one of Luke's favorite words; he uses it much more than the other Gospel writers. It means deliverance from all manner of ills, for the Greek word *soteria* can mean "salvation," "deliverance," and "healing." Perhaps Luke the physician liked to see Jesus' work as the ultimate fulfillment of his own calling.

Lived in the desert (1:80). John's parents were old when he was born and probably died soon afterwards. There were several communities of religious Jews in the wilderness of Judea between Jerusalem and the Dead Sea.[5]

6. Zechariah's prophecy in Luke 1:68-79 is called the Benedictus, Latin for "praise be." For what character qualities and acts does Zechariah praise God?

_____

_____

_____

_____

_____

_____

7. How does 1:68-79 further reveal . . .

John's mission? _____

_____

_____

_____

_____

_____

Jesus' mission? _____

_____

_____

_____

_____

_____

Optional Application:
a. Does 1:74-75 have any implications for your prayer or priorities? If so, what are they?
b. How is Jesus' mission as Savior of the world relevant to your current situation? Meditate on what it means for Jesus to be Savior—"If Jesus is my Savior, then . . . ."

8. Zechariah said that the Lord would rescue the Jews because of the covenant (pact, treaty) He had made with their ancestors (1:72-73). What would be the ultimate goal of this deliverance and this covenant (1:74-75)?

_____

_____

_____

_____

_____

_____

Jesus' birth (2:1-20)

Luke 2:1 puts these events into the context of world history. God used a Roman emperor to fulfill the plan He announced in Micah 5:2. This census probably occurred sometime between 6 and 4 BC.

Joseph and Mary had a three-day trip from Nazareth to Bethlehem. It must have seemed miserable timing to the woman—nine months pregnant and riding a donkey or walking all day in the dust and weather. Possibly not every family had to return to ancestral homes; Joseph may have had property in Bethlehem.[6]

Manger (2:7). A feeding trough for animals.

Cloth (2:7). Newborn babies were normally wrapped to make them feel secure. The cloths also helped to prevent babies' soft limbs from being distorted.[7]

Shepherds (2:8). They were classed with prostitutes and tax collectors as scum because 1) they could not keep the ceremonial law, which restricted, for example, the touching of dead things; and 2) they traveled around with loose habits, no fixed residence, and few scruples about other people's property. Considered untrustworthy, shepherds were forbidden to testify in court.

Despite this stereotype, however, these shepherds already may have been devout or ready to hear the good news. It is significant that God chose to announce His Son's birth to real shepherds rather than to the religious and civil leaders, who were supposed to be His people's shepherds longing for the Messiah (Ezekiel 34:1-31).[8]

9. Why did God have His Son born in the circumstances described in 2:7, rather than in a royal or at least comfortable household? (See Luke 6:20, 9:58, 22:27; 2 Corinthians 8:9.)

_____

_____

_____

_____

_____

_____

10. What does 2:1-20 reveal about . . .

Jesus' identity (2:11)?

_____

_____

_____

_____

How people and angels responded to His coming (2:14-20)?

_____

_____

_____

_____

_____

For Thought and Discussion: What was God saying by having His Son's birth announced to such people as shepherds, rather than to the nation's official shepherds (leaders) or at least to people considered respectable? See Luke 5:32; 6:20,24; 11:46-52.

For Thought and Discussion: What did the angels mean by proclaiming peace to those whom God favored?

For Thought and Discussion:
a. To whom does God assure peace in 2:14? Why to them? (Consider Proverbs 16:7.)
b. Trace the idea of God's pleasure in 3:2, 10:21, 12:32.

For Further Study: Compare 2:10-14 with Isaiah 9:6.

Optional Application: The Son of God was born in a stable. What implications does this fact have for the way you view your own situation? Talk to God about this.

35

For Further Study:
The teachers with whom Jesus talked in the Temple (2:46) were rabbis discussing interpretations of the Law and the Prophets (two of the three main sections of the Old Testament). What attitude toward the Law did Jesus show in this episode?

For Thought and Discussion: How is Jesus a model for Christian children in 2:40,49,51?

Optional Application: From the prophecies in chapters 1 and 2, describe at least one way in which Jesus' coming affects you— your life, your needs, your present, your future, your relationships.

Jesus presented in the Temple (2:21-40)

Purification (2:22). A mother was ritually unclean for forty days after bearing a son; on the fortieth day she brought a sacrifice to the Temple (Leviticus 12:1-8). Contact with symbols of life and death— corpses, semen, menstrual blood, birthing— demanded separation from holy things (Leviticus 15). Joseph and Jesus were probably also unclean from having touched Mary. Mary's sacrifice (Luke 2:24) was the smallest permitted, that of a poor person.

This utter separation between the Creator who is eternal spirit and creatures that are born physically was deeply ingrained in the Jews. The belief that the Holy Lord had become a human woman's baby seemed blasphemous to most Jews.

Present him (2:22). Every firstborn belonged to God; he either had to be ransomed with a fee or offered to God (Exodus 13:2,12-13). If offered, he crossed the barrier between the common and the holy (1 Samuel 1:11,22,28). Jesus was evidently offered to become holy, set apart for God's service.

11. What do you learn from 2:21-40 about . . .

Jesus' mission (2:30-35)? _____

_____

_____

_____

_____

How people responded to Him (2:28,38)? _____

_____

_____

_____

_____

Jesus at twelve (2:41-52)

The Law commanded adult males to attend three feasts each year: Passover, Pentecost (Weeks), and Tabernacles (Booths). (See Exodus 23:14-17, Deuteronomy 16:16.) Distance hindered many people, but most tried to be in Jerusalem for Passover.

At twelve, Jesus had one more year until He would be considered an adult responsible for keeping the Law. On this trip He would have been preparing to participate in the ceremonies the next year.

Jews normally referred to God as "Our Father" or "Our Father in heaven." As early as twelve, Jesus passed over this formal address to say "my Father" (Luke 2:49), a child's familiar term for his daddy (compare 11:2).

12. What does 2:40-52 reveal about . . .

Jesus' identity (2:49)? _____

_____

_____

_____

_____

Jesus' character (2:40,43-47,49,51-52)? _____

_____

_____

_____

13. a. What does Luke say about the *content* of the good news in 1:5–2:52? (See 1:11-17,26-35, 50-55,68-79; 2:11,14,30-32,34-35.)

_____

_____

_____

_____

For Further Study:
What do you learn about the Holy Spirit from the following verses: 1:15,35,41,67; 2:25,27?

For Further Study:
Luke tried to show in his Gospel that everything in history happens according to God's plan. How do chapters 1 and 2 reflect this theme? (See, for instance, 2:1-3.)

37

_____

_____

_____

b. Summarize the *response* people made to the
good news in these chapters. (See 1:18,38,
42-47,67-68; 2:17,20,28,38.)

_____

_____

_____

_____

_____

_____

14. Prayerfully consider whether anything in 1:5–2:52
has implications for your life today. Think about the
Optional Applications in this lesson, as well as anything else that impressed you.

a. What one insight from this lesson would you like
to focus on for application this week?

_____

_____

_____

b. Write down at least one way in which this insight
is relevant to your actions toward God, other
people, or circumstances.

_____

_____

_____

c. What one concrete step can you take (consistent prayer, a decision, a change of attitude toward circumstances, action, etc.) in light of this insight?

_____

_____

_____

Optional Application: Think about the responses people made to the good news. Do any of them suggest ways you might respond to 1:5–2:52? What practical steps could you take to follow the examples of the people Luke describes?

15. List any questions you have about anything in this lesson.

_____

_____

_____

_____

Peace on Earth

The Roman emperor Caesar Augustus (Luke 2:1) brought the *Pax Romana* ("Roman Peace") to the Mediterranean world in 27 BC. The Roman Peace meant that the empire's people were secure from invasion and safe to travel and trade freely.

However, to the people of Judea there was no peace as long as Roman soldiers occupied their land and Roman tax collectors took their money. The Jews hoped for a Messiah who would liberate them politically and make them a strong nation (Isaiah 9:2-7, 11:4; Luke 1:68-74)—this was their idea of the "Prince of Peace" (Isaiah 9:6).

But "peace" meant much more than political security to the Old Testament prophets. The Jews were correct in believing that the Roman Peace was no true peace, but they were wrong in reading prophecies selectively. The promised "peace" of the Messiah meant wholeness and wellness in all of creation—reconciliation between God and man, psychological rest and health, physical wholeness, social harmony, abundant harvest, and also political security. All the latter aspects of peace would grow from the former; God would end the enmity between Himself and man, and His presence would heal all other hurts.[9]

39

1. Morris, page 26; Marshall, page 46.
2. Michael Wilcock, *Savior of the World: The Message of Luke's Gospel* (Downer's Grove, Ill.: InterVarsity Press, 1979), pages 39-40.
3. The beginning of Herod's reign is given as 37 BC in *The NIV Study Bible*, page 1535; and Henry E. Dosker, "Herod," *The International Standard Bible Encyclopedia*, volume 3, edited by James Orr (Grand Rapids, Mich.: William B. Eerdmans Publishing Company, 1956), page 1379. The date is 40 BC according to Marshall, page 51; and R.E. Nixon, "Matthew," *The New Bible Commentary: Revised*, edited by Donald Guthrie, et al. (Grand Rapids, Mich.: William B. Eerdmans Publishing Company, 1970), page 818.
4. Morris, page 69.
5. *The NIV Study Bible*, page 1538.
6. Marshall, pages 101-105.
7. W. H. Van Doren, *The Gospel of Luke* (Grand Rapids, Mich.: Kregel Publications, 1981), page 50.
8. Morris, page 84.
9. Hartmut Beck and Colin Brown, "Peace," *The New International Dictionary of New Testament Theology*, volume 2, edited by Colin Brown (Grand Rapids, Mich.: Zondervan Corporation, 1976), pages 776-783.

Luke 3:1–4:13

The Preparation

Luke's Gospel is no biography; in an instant we leap twenty years, and the children of 1:1–2:52 are grown men. The cousins—Son and prophet of the Most High (1:32,76)—meet for perhaps the first time since the womb (1:41).

Before beginning the questions, read all of 3:1–4:13, thinking about the content and response of the good news and the purpose of Luke's book. Then skim all the questions in the lesson before you start to answer any. This preparation will help refresh your memory of the whole passage and will show you where the lesson is going.

John's message (3:1-20)

Luke 3:1-2 dates the beginning of John's ministry. The verses set the story in the context of the political history which God had prepared for the advent of His Son. (See the timeline on page 18.)

Tiberias (3:1). Scholars disagree over when his reign began. His fifteenth year was sometime between AD 25 and 29.[1]

Herod (3:1). Herod the Great was king when Jesus and John were born (1:5); his son Herod Antipas and two other sons succeeded him in 4 BC. Herod

For Further Study:
Repentance (3:3) is
literally a "turning
around." Using a
dictionary if necessary,
explain what it means to
repent of sin.

Antipas is the Herod in 3:1 and the rest of the
Gospel. He ruled Galilee and Perea from 4 BC to
AD 39.

Tetrarch (3:1). Officially, Herod was a "tetrarch," the
ruler of one-fourth of Palestine. Ordinary people in
Galilee and Rome called him "king" (Matthew
14:1, Mark 6:14).[2]

Annas . . . Caiaphas (3:2). Officially, there was only
one high priest at a time. However, the issue had
been confused ever since Rome began to appoint
high priests to assure their loyalty. Annas was high
priest from AD 6 to 15, when the emperor replaced
him with his son Eleazar. Another son, Caiphas,
was appointed high priest from AD 18 to 37. However, "Jews regarded the high priesthood as a life-
office" whatever Rome did, so they still considered
Annas to be the real high priest. John 18:13-24
shows that Annas retained "considerable power
behind the scenes."[3]

1. Luke gives a vivid sense of John's character through
dialogue. What did John tell the people to do?

3:3 _____

_____

_____

_____

3:8 _____

_____

_____

_____

Baptism (3:3) John's baptism was a new application of
a familiar practice. Jews baptized converts because
they regarded all Gentiles as needing to be
cleansed from sin. John shocked people by claiming that even Jews needed to be cleansed.

Prepare the way (3:4). In ancient times, a herald
would travel ahead of a royal procession, announc-
ing the king's coming and commanding
preparations.

2. What reasons did John give for the instructions you
listed in question 1?

3:3 _____

_____

_____

_____

3:4-6 _____

_____

_____

_____

3:7,9 _____

_____

_____

_____

_____

> **Optional Application:**
> Repentance includes
> attitudes as well as
> actions. Consider the
> attitude John
> condemned in 3:8. How
> might a Christian be
> tempted to have a
> similar wrong attitude?

Tax collectors (3:12). These men were hated both as
collaborators (they collected for the hated Roman
occupiers) and as extortioners (Rome hired them
to collect a fixed amount, and any percentage
more than this that they could extract was their
profit).

Soldiers (3:14). These were also privileged, powerful,
and disliked.

For Thought and Discussion: How would the actions John urged help a person to "prepare the way for the Lord"?

For Further Study: What did John say about the Holy Spirit (3:16-17)?

3. a. John did not tell tax collectors or soldiers to change jobs, but he did tell them how to "produce fruit in keeping with repentance." What did he say (3:12-14)?

_____

_____

_____

_____

_____

b. Does 3:12-14 offer us a general principle for business conduct, for behavior in the workplace? If so, what is it?

_____

_____

_____

_____

_____

4. John told tax collectors and soldiers to act with *justice* at work. However, what standard did John tell the crowd to apply in their private lives as fruit of repentance (3:11)

_____

_____

_____

_____

44

5. Write down one way in which the standard of 3:11 applies to your life and one way in which the business ethic of 3:12-14 applies.

Optional Application: Does question 5 suggest any action or change of attitude you need to make?

Private standard _____

_____

_____

_____

_____

_____

Business ethic _____

_____

_____

_____

_____

_____

6. Summarize what John prophesied about the "one" who was coming (3:16-17).

_____

_____

_____

_____

7. In what way was John's message "good news" (3:18)?

_____

_____

Optional Application:
John commends justice in professional life, but in private life he commands love— generous self-sacrifice that goes beyond what you owe someone. Paul makes a similar point in Romans 13:8-10. How could group members put John's description of self-sacrifice (Luke 3:11) into practice?

For Thought and Discussion: Jesus had never rebelled against the Father's will for His life (Luke 22:42, John 15:10), so He did not need to be baptized for repentance. Why then was Jesus baptized (Matthew 3:14-15; John 1:31-34, 2 Corinthians 5:21, Hebrews 2:17)?

For Further Study: At what other occasions did the Father speak from heaven about Jesus (Luke 9:35, John 12:28)?

For Further Study: The meanings of baptism with the Holy Spirit and fire and of the burning of the chaff (Luke 3:16-17) are debated. Acts 2:1-41 and 1 Corinthians 3:13 may help your group interpret these things.

_____

_____

_____

8. Does any insight from 3:1-20 suggest a course of action you want to take or a matter you want to pray about? If so, describe what you plan to do.

_____

_____

_____

_____

_____

Jesus' baptism (3:21-22)

9. Jesus' baptism was important for many reasons. What did the Father publicly declare about Jesus at His baptism (3:22)?

_____

_____

_____

10. What did the Holy Spirit do (3:22)?

_____

_____

_____

Jesus' genealogy (3:23-38)

Matthew begins his Gospel with Jesus' genealogy traced down from Abraham through David and Joseph. Jesus was Joseph's legal son in Jewish eyes, even though Joseph was not the biological father. Matthew's purpose is to show the Jews that Jesus is the legal heir of David's kingship and Abraham's covenant.

By contrast, Luke is less concerned to prove to his Gentile audience that Jesus is the King of Israel. Luke traces Jesus' inheritance back through Joseph (His legal father), Heli (Mary's father—Joseph's father-in-law and so his adopted father by Jewish law; compare Luke 3:23-31 to Matthew 1:12-16), David, Abraham, Adam, and God. By following Jesus' biological line, Luke stresses two key facts: Jesus is truly son of Adam, fully human; and Jesus is truly Son of God, the only son of Adam who retains the image of God unmarred by the Fall.

At His baptism, the sinless son of Adam identified with all other men who need God's cleansing, and He was acclaimed Son of God, the Father's only pleasing Son. Now Luke inserts a genealogy to show that Jesus was fully son of Adam and Son of God long before that acclamation.

Jesus' temptations (4:1-13)

Immediately after identifying with man in baptism, Jesus goes into the wilderness to be tempted as a man. Having been declared Son of God and filled with the Holy Spirit (3:22, 4:1), Jesus is tempted concerning His submission to the Father and the Spirit.

The Old Testament passages Jesus quotes are from Deuteronomy 8:3 and 6:13,16. This section of Deuteronomy discusses Israel's time of being tested by God in the wilderness. Israel largely failed the test of utter loyalty to God (Deuteronomy 6:4-5, 9:7; Jeremiah 31:31-32). God tested Israel, but the devil tempts Jesus with the Holy Spirit's permission.

Test (4:12). To make someone prove his love, faithfulness, or ability. See Exodus 17:1-4.

---

11. One purpose of Jesus' baptism was that He might identify fully with man. How did His temptation fulfill a similar purpose (Hebrews 2:18, 4:15)?

_____

_____

_____

_____

hungry
angry
lonely
tired
} open to temptation

47

For Thought and Discussion: What conclusions about temptation in our own lives can we draw from the facts that Jesus was tempted by the devil . . .

a. while He was being led by the Spirit (4:1-2)?

b. while He was fasting and praying in preparation for His ministry (4:14-15)?

12. a. In all three temptations, Satan intended to entice Jesus to grasp by His own power what the Father planned to give in His own time (Philippians 2:6-9). In what specific area was Jesus asked to disobey His Father in each of the three temptations?

4:3-4 _____

_____

_____

_____

_____

4:5-8 _____

_____

_____

_____

_____

4:9-12 _____

_____

_____

_____

b. Are you tempted to grasp at anything that God would give by grace in His own time? Or, are you facing some other temptation? Ask God to show you one particular area of temptation, and then describe it.

_____

_____

_____

_____

_____

13. a. What equipment did Jesus use to defend Himself against temptation (4:1,4,8,12)?

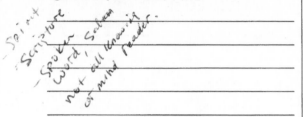

   b. Did the Son of God use any weapons against temptation that are unavailable to us? What are the implications of this fact for us?

14. How could you apply Jesus' weapons against the temptation you described in question 12b?

15. a. In summary, what does 3:1–4:13 reveal about the content of the good news (John's message and Jesus' identity, mission, and character)? See 3:3-6,22,38; 4:4,8,12.

Optional Application: Using a topical Bible or concordance, search the Scriptures for passages (such as 1 Corinthians 10:13) that could strengthen you in the temptation that currently confronts you.

For Further Study: Compare Paul's definition of justice in Romans 13:7 ("Give everyone what you owe him") to what John proclaimed. How does this apply to you? How are you tempted to take more than you deserve in your work?

For Thought and Discussion: In the temptation of Jesus, the Savior both fulfills another crucial step on the way to completing His mission and gives us an example for dealing with temptation. How did Jesus reveal Himself to us in the temptation? How did He set an example for us?

49

b. How would you summarize the way this section encourages us to respond to the good news? See 3:8,11-14; 4:4,8,12.

_____

_____

_____

_____

_____

16. List any questions you have about 3:1–4:13.

_____

_____

_____

_____

_____

The Baptism of Jesus

This event is important for several reasons:

1. Jesus was consecrated (set apart) for ministry.

2. The Father and the Spirit officially approved Jesus to fulfill His mission. God declared that Jesus met His righteous requirements to be the Savior of the world.

3. John the Baptist announced the arrival of the Messiah and the beginning of His ministry (John 1:29-34).

4. Jesus identified with man's need to be cleansed from sin (2 Corinthians 5:21).

5. Jesus set an example of baptism for His followers.[4]

1. Marshall, page 133; _The NIV Study Bible_, pages 1540-1541.
2. _The NIV Study Bible_, page 1463.
3. Marshall, page 134.
4. _The NIV Study Bible_, page 1446.

Luke 4:14–5:39

Galilean Ministry Begins

Baptized in water, filled with the Holy Spirit, and armed with God's Word against temptations, Jesus is ready to begin His ministry—but very quickly He runs into opposition. The people expect the son of Joseph; they get the Son of God. They want Him to satisfy their hopes; He exposes their beliefs as contrary to God's character.

Jesus shocks the religious establishment by acknowledging Gentiles, forgiving sin, and eating with sinners. He refuses to teach and heal according to men's ideas. In fact, far from avoiding confrontation, Jesus' teachings and actions consistently collide with traditional views. And yet a number of men see in Him something unusual and become His disciples.

Read 4:14–5:39, looking for Jesus' impact on everyone around Him.

At Nazareth (4:14-30)

Between the temptation's end in 4:13 and the events at Nazareth in 4:16-30 lay months of preaching and healing throughout Galilee. Luke knew that much ministry preceded the sermon at Nazareth (Luke 4:14-15,23), but he put the Nazareth incident at the head of his story as a symbol of the nation's rejection of Jesus.[1]

Luke 4:16-30 "is the oldest known account of a synagogue service."[2] Distinguished visitors often were invited to read from Scripture and give an interpretation. Since Jesus returned to Nazareth as a local boy who had made a name for Himself in a nearby town

51

Optional Application:
In what ways are you in
need of the ministry
Jesus announced in
4:18-19? Ask Him to do
these things in your life.

(Luke 4:14-15), it was fitting that He should be invited
to give the Sabbath address.

There was probably no fixed schedule of prophetic
readings at this time,[3] as there was for the Law. The
ruler may have selected the prophetic passage, or he
may have left Jesus full or partial freedom to choose
His text. In Nazareth He read Isaiah 61:1-2. This section of Isaiah includes several passages about the
"Servant of the Lord" who would save Israel.

1. Summarize the message Jesus announced in
   4:18-21.

   _____

   _____

   _____

   _____

Sat down (Luke 4:20). "It was customary to stand while
   reading Scripture (4:16) but to sit while teaching."[4]

2. In what sense was Isaiah 61:1-2 "fulfilled" in the
   hearing of Jesus' audience (Luke 4:21)?

   _____

   _____

   _____

3. a. Who did the Nazarenes think Jesus was? Who
      was He really (4:22; 1:35; 3:22,23,38; 4:3)?

   _____

   _____

   _____

   _____

b. Why was the Nazarenes' error crucial in light of the proclamation in 4:18-21?

_____

_____

_____

_____

_____

Elijah . . . Elisha (4:25-27). When God afflicted Israel for worshiping Baal, Elijah spent the drought not with a good Jewish widow but with a Phoenician widow near Sidon (1 Kings 16:29–17:24). Later, Elisha healed none of the lepers in Israel, but only Israel's arch-enemy, the Syrian military commander Naaman (2 Kings 5:1-27).

4. Jesus deliberately reminded the Nazarenes that He had been healing other people and that God had frequently blessed the scorned Gentiles. What did He want them—and us—to understand about God and His Kingdom?

_____

_____

_____

5. How would you describe Jesus' character from 4:14-30 (especially 4:21,23-27,30)?

_____

_____

_____

_____

Optional Application:
How can you acquire the peace in the face of threat that Jesus shows in 4:30? Consider meditating on God's promises and your relationship to Him.

For Thought and Discussion: According to Luke 11:20, what did Jesus' authority over demons prove?

At Capernaum (4:31-44)

After His rejection in Nazareth, Jesus returned to Capernaum, where He had been living for some time (Matthew 4:13). This fishing village on the shore of the Sea of Galilee was a good, central place for a home base. From there Jesus would take trips around Galilee, teaching in synagogues and the open countryside.

6. What did Jesus' spoken word accomplish in 4:32,35,39?

_____

_____

_____

_____

Authority and power (4:36). The Galileans had seen other traveling wonderworkers cast out demons; this was a rare but not unique talent. However, most exorcists required a long process of invoking power, arguing with the demon, extracting its name, and so on. By contrast, Jesus cut short the battle of will and issued a simple command (4:35).

7. Why were people amazed at Jesus' teaching (4:32; compare Mark 1:22)?

_____

_____

_____

8. Compare Jesus' word of preaching in Luke 4:18-21 to His word of power in 4:31-41. How were teaching and action related?

_____

_____

_____

_____

_____

_____

Optional Application:
Tell someone the good news about Jesus that you've studied in 4:14-44.

The kingdom of God (4:43). This phrase occurs more than thirty times in Luke's Gospel. It has many meanings, including: "the eternal kingship of God; the presence of the kingdom in the person of Jesus, the King; the approaching spiritual form of the kingdom; the future kingdom."[5] In other words, the Kingdom of God "is the rule of God and is both a present reality and a future hope."[6]

Optional Application:
Reflect on the connection between Jesus' peace (4:30), authority (4:32,36), and prayer (4:42). Ask God how you could more fully follow Jesus' example in this matter. Spend some time with Him.

9. Jesus said His ministry was to "preach the good news [*euangelizesthai*] of the kingdom of God" (4:43). What do you learn about the Kingdom from 4:14-41?

_____

_____

_____

_____

The first disciples called (5:1-11)

All night (5:5). That was the normal time for deep-sea fishing.[7] Simon knew that fishing during the day would be useless.

Study Skill—Observing and Interpreting
To study a scene in a Gospel, begin by noticing every detail, even the seemingly trivial—there was a lake called Gennesaret; Jesus spoke to crowds; etc. From these observations, decide which are the key words in the scene.

10. Simon knew that Jesus was no fisherman, but he had enough respect for the teacher not to scoff

a. Jesus really got Simon's attention when He demonstrated His authority not just in religious matters, but over fish. Why do you think authority over fish affected Simon so much more profoundly?

b. What kind of authority would get your attention that strongly?

Optional Application:

a. Have you ever seen Jesus' authority over all of life as Simon did? If so, how did the experience affect you?

b. Meditate this week on Jesus' authority and the response He asks of you. How could you act on 5:10-11?

when Jesus suggested fishing at an absurd time (5:4-5). How did Jesus prove to Simon that He had authority over more than religious things (5:6-10)?

_____

_____

_____

_____

A leper cleansed (5:12-16)

Leprosy (5:12). In biblical times, leprosy included several skin diseases, such as skin cancers, herpes, and the illness we call leprosy. Some of the diseases were hideous to see and smell, but all lepers were quarantined and survived only on charity. Their sickness was considered punishment for sin, and it barred them from human contact and religious worship. Anyone who touched a leper was thereby unclean and so had to avoid people and worship for a time. A person was not "healed" from leprosy, but "cleansed" as from sin or other filth.

Priest (5:14). Only the priests, acting as health inspectors, could certify a person clean of leprosy. The person then offered sacrifice in thanksgiving and was readmitted to human society and Jewish worship (Leviticus 13-14).

_____

11. What did Jesus' willingness to actually touch the leper show about Jesus' character?

_____

_____

_____

_____

_____

_____

A paralytic healed (5:17-26)

Observe how differently the religious authorities responded to Jesus.

Pharisees (5:17). There were only about six thousand Pharisees in Palestine—one percent of the population.[8] Still, they were an influential party because people respected them as the "unofficial religious leaders."[9] They believed that obedience to God's commands was the most important religious attitude, so in order to avoid unintentionally breaking a command, they "fenced" the Law with interpretations. For instance, to avoid using God's name in vain, they never used it. These interpretations of the Law had been handed down as traditions for generations, so they were regarded as equally authoritative as Scripture itself.[10]

Teachers of the law (5:17). These men, also called "scribes," interpreted and taught both the written Law of Scripture and the oral law of tradition. Most of the teachers belonged to the party of the Pharisees.[11]

Blasphemy (5:21). Pharisees considered this the worst sin a person could commit. It included any offense to God's authority or majesty. According to Jewish theology, not even the Messiah could forgive sins, so Jesus was claiming the authority of God alone.[12]

---

12. According to 5:20, why did Jesus declare the paralytic's sins forgiven?

_____

_____

_____

13. Jesus had a second reason for forgiving and healing the paralytic. What did His deeds prove, and how did they prove it (5:21-26)?

_____

_____

For Thought and Discussion: Jesus told the man to follow the legal requirements for certifying that he had been cured. What testimony (5:14) would this bear to the priests and the nation?

For Thought and Discussion: Was the faith Jesus commended (5:20) necessary for forgiveness of sins? Why or why not?

For Thought and Discussion: What must the Pharisees have believed (about God, sin, righteousness) that made them consider it wrong to eat with sinners (5:30)?

Jesus and sinners (5:27-32)

Levi collected customs duties outside town. He was employed by someone who had bid for the job from Rome. Levi's apostolic name was Matthew (Matthew 9:9), just as Simon's apostolic name was Peter.[13]

Sinners (5:30). The Pharisees applied this label to tax collectors, robbers, adulterers, prostitutes, shepherds, and anyone else who did not follow the Law according to the interpretations of the elders.[14]

---

14. Levi's decision to abandon his toll booth meant permanently leaving his job. What does Levi's choice show about discipleship (5:27-28)?

15. What do Jesus' words to the Pharisees reveal about His mission (5:31-32)?

16. Think about what Jesus does in 5:1-32 and how each person responds. How would you summarize what this passage contributes to the message of the gospel? See 5:10,20,24,29,31-32.

_____

_____

_____

Fasting versus feasting (5:33-39)

Jesus and His disciples feasted because they wanted to be where sinners were (5:29-32)—but there was a deeper reason for their choice as well.

_____

Disciples (5:33). The followers of a rabbi (master, teacher). A disciple in rabbinic Judaism was bound closely to his master. The master was the disciple's sole authority for truth and model for life. However, Jesus took the relationship beyond Jewish tradition, requiring that His disciples' allegiance to Him surpassed their allegiance to family, the Law, and even life itself (6:5, 14:26-27).[15]

Fast and pray (5:33). All Jews fasted yearly on the Day of Atonement (Leviticus 16:29). Individuals chose to fast at other times for worship or prayer; both the Pharisees and John's disciples did so frequently. Jesus fasted in the desert (4:2) and after the Last Supper (22:16,18).

Wineskins (5:37). Wine was kept in goatskin bags. "As the fresh grape juice fermented, the wine would expand, and the new wineskin would stretch. But a used skin, already stretched, would break."[16]

For Thought and Discussion: Why was fasting inappropriate while Jesus was present?

17. Old garments tear when patched, and old wineskins break when refilled. Why do you think people sometimes prefer to patch their old coats or keep their old wineskins?

Comfort, habit, taste
don't have to make
changes - consistency

18. What one truth from 4:14–5:39 would you most like to apply? Write it down, with a verse reference.

19. List any questions you have about 4:14–5:39.

1. Wilcock, pages 60-61.
2. Marshall, page 181.
3. Morris, page 106.
4. *The NIV Study Bible,* page 1545.
5. *The NIV Study Bible,* page 1546.
6. *The NIV Study Bible,* page 1444.
7. Marshall, page 202.
8. F.F. Bruce, *New Testament History* (Garden City, N. Y. Doubleday, 1980), page 39 estimates the population of Palestine as 500,000 to 1.5 million. We don't know how many were Jews and how many were Gentiles. *The NIV Study Bible,* page 1547, says there were 6,000 Pharisees.
9. Morris, page 116.
10. *The NIV Study Bible,* page 1547.
11. *The NIV Study Bible,* page 1547.
12. *The NIV Study Bible,* pages 1495, 1527, 1547-1548.
13. *The NIV Study Bible,* page 1496.
14. *The NIV Study Bible,* page 1496.
15. Dietrich Muller, "Disciple," *The New International Dictionary of New Testament Theology,* volume 1, pages 480-490.
16. *The NIV Study Bible,* page 1455.

Luke 6–7

Kingdom People

Like Moses, Jesus ascended a mountain to be with God and descended to declare His Law (Luke 6:12,17).[1] But the "new commandment" (John 13:34), "the royal law" (James 2:8), was not like the old.

The standards of the Kingdom led Jesus to heal, forgive, embrace, reconcile, and celebrate with all comers. He also spelled out the laws of the Kingdom more fully.

Now let's look at the response that Jesus sought to the message of salvation. Read chapters 6 and 7.

The Sabbath (6:1-11)

Unlawful (6:2). To the Pharisees, the command to rest on the Sabbath had become a rule to prove one's obedience to God. To assure that no one violated the Fourth Commandment, the rabbis had specified every possible action permitted or forbidden on that day. They made picking, rubbing, and eating even a few grains equivalent to reaping, threshing, and preparing food—all manifestly work.

What David did (Luke 6:3). When David and his men were hungry, they accepted holy bread from the Tabernacle (1 Samuel 21:1-9) even though it was unlawful for anyone but the priests to eat it (Leviticus 24:5-9).

For Further Study:
Compare Luke 6:1-11 to
Isaiah 58:6-7,13.

For Further Study:
Make a list of all the
things the Pharisees
wanted Jesus to do or
not do that Jesus
rejected. Then list why
each thing is or isn't
appropriate for the
kingdom.

Optional Application:
How can you celebrate
God's Sabbath of rest
and liberation, a
foretaste of the
Kingdom?

1. According to the Pharisees, a person should go
   hungry rather than glean on the Sabbath (Luke
   6:1-2). How did this view of God's Sabbath miss its
   true significance?

   rules v. relationship

   it is possible to be a

   "rules follower" and still miss

   the mark

2. Jesus defended not only His motives but also His
   authority to let His disciples glean on the Sabbath
   (6:5). What did He claim, and why was His claim
   significant?

   He was the lord of the

   Sabbath

The Twelve (6:12-16)

Apostle (6:13). "One who is sent," a herald, ambassador,
   or proxy. The Twelve were going to be Jesus' special
   representatives to the world as well as the leaders of
   His church. After Jesus' death, others in the church,
   such as Paul, were recognized as apostles.

Zealot (6:15). There were four main parties within
   Judaism in Jesus' time: Pharisees, Sadducees,
   Essenes, and Zealots. The Zealots were so passion-
   ate about God's lordship over the Jews that they
   considered it unlawful to acknowledge the sover-
   eignty of Gentile rulers. Therefore, they opposed
   paying taxes to Rome (20:22) and often rioted
   when a census was taken for tax purposes. The

Zealots felt called actively to help God liberate Israel.[2] According to the Jewish historian Josephus, in the 50s AD Zealots systematically assassinated many Jewish leaders who cooperated with Rome, for they were as opposed to oppression from rich Jews as they were to Roman occupation.[3]

Iscariot (6:16). This probably means "the man from Kerioth,"[4] a town in Judea. Judas may have been the only Judean among the apostles.

Kingdom values (6:17-26)

Crowds of both Jews and Gentiles come from as far away as Sidon to see Jesus (6:17). Notice why they come (6:18-19).

Blessed (6:20). "Happy," "joyful," not because of luck or fortune, but because of divine favor, particularly salvation.[5]

Woe (6:24). "Alas"; this word expresses "pity for those who stand under judgment,"[6] compassion, not an angry threat.

3. Jesus begins His sermon by contrasting two kinds of people (6:20-26). He discusses each in four parallel ways.

a. Who is blessed, and why?

_____

_____

_____

_____

_____

b. Who is pitiable, and why?

_____

_____

For Thought and Discussion: What attitudes (toward self, the world, God) tempt rich and respected people to lose the greatest blessing? (Optional: **See** Deuteronomy 8:17-18; 9:4; Luke 8:14; 12:21,34.)

4. Why is the Kingdom given to disciples who are poor and rejected for Jesus' sake, while people who are rich and respected are in grave danger?

The law of love (6:27-42)

Having turned the world's values upside down, Jesus proceeds to overturn the world's standard of fairness.

But I tell you (6:27). The Law of Moses laid down the rights and duties of justice—what each person owed another. Jesus does not reject the Mosaic definition of justice, but in private relations between individuals, Jesus lays down a new law.

---

5. In general, what is Jesus' rule for life (6:27-36)?

6. From 6:27-36, explain what you think it means to love your enemies. (What is love? Who are your enemies?)

_____

_____

_____

_____

Optional Application:
What "measure" (6:38) do you use in evaluating and treating family members, friends, coworkers, etc.? In what ways might you need to change the standard by which you measure out love, judgment, giving, and forgiveness?

Study Skill—Context

It is crucial to read individual commands in light of the whole passage, the entire book, and the rest of Scripture. The command, "Do not judge" (Luke 6:37) is a good example. Elsewhere, Jesus commands us to discern right from wrong in ourselves and others (Matthew 7:15-20; Luke 6:43-45, 7:43, 12:57; compare Acts 4:19). Therefore, we must understand the word "judge" in light of Luke 6:27-36. Here, to judge is to pass judgment on someone, to declare what he justly deserves, and furthermore to wish heartily that he will get what is coming to him. Jesus warns against judging that someone is your enemy, that he deserves to be hated and punished for hating, cursing, mistreating, striking, or robbing you (6:27-29). Context also shows us that judgment and condemnation are the opposites of love, mercy, giving, and forgiving.

---

7. What principle does Jesus reveal in 6:37-38 about why we should treat others as we would like to be treated?

_____

_____

_____

_____

_____

Optional Application:
Evaluate your own heart
by the standard of 6:45.
What areas of your heart
need forgiveness and
cleansing?

**For Thought and
Discussion:** Observe
what Jesus says about
obedience to His Law
(6:46-49). How is
obeying Jesus like
building your house on a
rock?

For Further Study:
Compare Luke 7:11-17
to 1 Kings 17:9,17-24.
How did Jesus' act
resemble Elijah's? Why
do you think people
responded as they did to
Jesus' act (Luke 7:16)?

8. What will happen if we try to be our brother's spiritual guide and judge while we are blind to our own
weaknesses (6:39)?

_____

_____

_____

_____

Integrity (6:43-49)

9. With the warnings of 6:37-42 in mind, how can we
recognize the state of our hearts (6:43-45)?

_____

_____

_____

_____

_____

A centurion and his servant (7:1-10)

Centurion (7:2). Roughly equivalent to an army cap-
tain. He commanded a company of a hundred
troops, in this case probably for Herod the
tetrarch.[7]

10. Scripture records only two occasions on which
Jesus was "amazed" (Mark 6:6, Luke 7:9). What
was it about the centurion that so amazed Jesus?

_____

_____

_____

_____

A woman and her son (7:11-17)

Widow (7:12). A woman without any men to protect her was the most helpless of people, since wage work for women was rare.

11. Why did Jesus raise the young man (7:13)?

_____

_____

_____

_____

12. Jesus' good news is for "the poor." Who are the poor who receive Jesus' ministry in 7:1-10? In 7:11-17?

_____

_____

_____

_____

13. What is the "good news of the kingdom" that Jesus brings to these people?

_____

_____

_____

_____

_____

Jesus answers John (7:18-23)

Are you the one (7:19). John's doubt is understandable. He was imprisoned shortly after he baptized Jesus (3:19-20), so he could know only what he heard.

For Thought and Discussion: How is Luke 7:22-23 an encouragement for believers awaiting the fulfillment of the Kingdom?

67

Optional Application:
With which debtor do
you identify in 7:41-42?
How should this parable
affect your attitude
toward God? How can
you act on that attitude
this week?

Isaiah had prophesied that the Messiah would "proclaim freedom for the prisoners" (Isaiah 61:1, Luke
4:18), but John was still in prison. Isaiah had said
the Messiah would "proclaim . . . the day of
vengeance of our God" (Isaiah 61:2), but John had
seen no vengeance on wicked men like Herod.

---

14. How did Jesus confirm His identity to John (Luke
   7:21-22)?

_____

_____

_____

_____

15. Compare Isaiah 61:2 to Luke 4:19. What part of Isaiah 61:2 was Jesus fulfilling, and what part was He
   leaving for His future return?

   Fulfilling in current ministry _____

   _____

   _____

   _____

   Leaving for future return _____

   _____

   _____

   _____

A sinful woman (7:36-50)

A woman who had lived a sinful life (7:37). A prostitute. She could easily have entered Simon's house,
   since dinners were not private. But she would not
   have been welcome.

At his feet (7:38). "People did not sit at the table, but
   reclined on low couches, leaning on the left arm

68

with the head toward the table and the body stretched away from it. The sandals were removed before reclining."[8] Therefore, the woman could not reach Jesus' head, the part of the body that a host normally anointed when a guest entered his house. But she could reach His feet, which were considered the meanest part of the body. The lowest servant of the household had the job of washing street dirt from guests' feet when they arrived.

Hair (7:38). Considered the most glorious part of the body. A woman almost never unbound her hair in public.[9]

For Thought and Discussion: How does Jesus' behavior in 7:36-50 fit with His normally humble character?

16. a. In the parable (7:41-42), what caused the man who was forgiven the five hundred denarii to love more than his fellow debtor?

> he owed more debt - the greater amount - would be harder to repay.

b. At the dinner (7:36-38,44-48), what caused the prostitute to show great love?

> She was a sinner - she adored Jesus - was unabashed in showing her love. She recognized who she was and who Jesus was.

c. Simon showed he loved Jesus little by the way he treated Jesus (7:39,44-46). According to 7:41-42, why did Simon love little?

> Simon believed his sin to be small, manageable (according to the parable) - therefore Jesus had little to offer him.

For Thought and Discussion: What do you learn about Jesus' definition of "the poor" who are blessed and "the rich" who are pitiable from 7:36-50? How does this incident illustrate why the poor are in better shape than the rich?

Optional Application: With whom can you share the most significant thing you learned from this lesson?

17. On what basis is the woman "forgiven" and "saved"?

"She loved much" she was wretched & broken and humbled herself before God

18. a. Who is "the poor" in 7:36-50, and how does that person display poverty?

Sinners who recognize their own sin and their inability to get from under it on their own (in their own) power. Wretched/broken

b. Who is "the rich" in this incident, and how does that person show it?

Simon? guests - using Jesus as a side-show. not recognizing the depths of their sin (debt)

c. What "good news of the kingdom" does the poor person receive from Jesus?

"Your sins are forgiven"
"Your faith has saved you"

70

Study Skill—Parables

Luke 7:41-42 is a classic parable; it is a little story, not a simple comparison. When trying to interpret a true parable, keep these guidelines in mind:

1. A true parable is like a joke in that the story has one main point that the hearer should catch at once. Jesus sets up an ordinary situation, then gives it an unexpected twist to make His point.

2. A parable is not meant to be a riddle or puzzle with a hidden meaning. Instead, just as you are meant to get the point of a joke and respond with laughter and perhaps a change of heart, so the point of a parable should hit you at once, startle you into looking at things differently, and move you to respond.

3. In order to "get" a joke about a traveling salesman, you have to know something about the culture and context. Likewise, in order to get the point of a parable, you have to understand relevant parts of Jewish culture during that time period.

4. A parable is not an allegory, where every element has symbolic meaning. Rather, it has "points of reference"[10] on which the story hinges and a single "point" that calls for a response.[11] The points of reference are chosen to draw the audience into the story so that they will respond when they get the point.

For instance, in Luke 7:41-42, the points of reference are the moneylender (symbolizing God) and the two debtors (Simon and the prostitute). The parable startles each hearer and demands a response: unloving Simon needs to repent of ingratitude toward God and scorn toward "sinners"; the loving prostitute needs to go in peace and joy, knowing that she is forgiven. For us, the question is, "Am I like Simon or the prostitute?"

For Thought and Discussion: John the Baptist was greatest among those "born of women" (Luke 7:28). Why is the least citizen of the Kingdom greater still (John 1:12-13, 3:5-8)?[12]

71

Jesus discusses John the Baptist
(7:24-35)

Remember that the visit from John's messengers prompted these comments from Jesus.

19. Why did the people reject John when he "sang a dirge" (7:32-33), when he lived strictly and preached warning?

_____

_____

_____

_____

20. Why did they reject Jesus when He "played the flute" (7:32,35), when He lived exuberantly and preached joy?

_____

_____

_____

_____

21. What further do you learn about being a disciple from Luke 6–7?

_____

_____

_____

_____

22. What questions do you have about Luke 6–7?

_____

_____

_____

_____

1. Wilcock, pages 78-79.
2. Bruce, page 96.
3. Bruce, pages 99-100.
4. Bruce, page 184.
5. Marshall, page 248.
6. Marshall, page 255.
7. *The NIV Study Bible*, page 1551.
8. Morris, page 147.
9. Morris, page 147.
10. Gordon D. Fee and Douglas Stuart, *How to Read the Bible for All Its Worth* (Grand Rapids, Mich.: Zondervan Corporation, 1982), page 127.
11. Fee and Stuart, page 126.
12. Luke 13:28 makes clear that John and the other Old Testament prophets and saints were going to enter the Kingdom of God along with the people who believed in Jesus after He came.

Luke 8–9

From Town to Town

In Luke 8–9 Jesus begins a second tour of the country-side.[1] His ministry in Galilee is drawing to a close. He has been a puzzle or an offense to most of His hearers, but a few have responded and become disciples. From now on, He will focus His efforts on training the disciples. On this last, long journey to Jerusalem, Jesus will work to equip His disciples to later preach the meaning of His life.

Read chapters 8–9, asking God to teach you what a disciple needs to know.

On the road (8:1-3)

Mary (called Magdalene) (8:2). Mary of Magdala has been equated with the prostitute of 7:36-50, but Luke makes it clear that Mary had been possessed by seven demons—a quite different trouble. Mary Magdalene should also not be confused with Mary of Bethany, the sister of Martha and Lazarus (John 11:1).

Helping to support them (8:3). Luke tells us more about women than Matthew, Mark, or John, and only Luke tells us how Jesus and His disciples were supported. In Jesus' day it was startling for a rabbi to let women support Him, but it was unheard-of for a rabbi to let women travel with him as disciples.[2]

Optional Application:
Think about the four
kinds of soil (8:11-15).
Which of them best
describes what most
hinders you from hearing
Jesus' word, responding,
and bearing a fruitful
crop? What can you do
about this problem?

**For Thought and
Discussion:** What does
it mean to have "a noble
and good heart" (8:15)?
How can a person
develop one?

**For Thought and
Discussion:** a. Jesus'
earthly ministry was a
mystery at the time. But
did He intend His
message to remain a
secret forever? Why or
why not (8:16-17)?
b. What implications
did this intention have
for Jesus' disciples, who
would be the only
people who understood
the secret once Jesus
left the world (8:16-18)?

The four soils (8:4-15)

1. What main point is Jesus trying to communicate in
this parable to the crowds who flocked around Him
(8:5-8,11-15)?

_____

_____

_____

_____

_____

_____

_____

To sow (8:5). "In Eastern practice the seed was sometimes sown first and the field plowed afterward.
Roads and pathways went directly through many
fields, and the traffic made much of the surface
too hard for seed to take root in."[3]

2. What kind of person does God enable to understand the puzzle of the Kingdom (8:9-10; compare
5:10-11, 7:50, 8:8)?

_____

_____

_____

_____

_____

_____

The lamp (8:16-18)

The original audience of the parable in 8:16 is the disciples, to whom the knowledge of God's secrets has been
given.

Jesus' true family (8:19-21)

3. Family was enormously important in Jewish culture, so Jesus' statement in 8:21 would have been shocking. Why do you think Jesus' true family are those who do what God's Word says?

_____

_____

_____

_____

_____

A storm (8:22-25)

Squall (8:23). The Sea of Galilee (Lake of Gennesaret) is thirteen by seven miles and lies about 700 feet below sea level. Cold winds often sweep down nearby mountains and whip up sudden storms.

4. a. What do the disciples learn about Jesus in 8:22-25?

_____

_____

_____

b. What do they learn about themselves?

_____

_____

_____

A demoniac (8:26-39)

Observe the pathetic plight of the possessed man in this scene (8:27-29).

For Thought and Discussion: a. Why must both inquirer and disciple take care to respond to whatever knowledge of God's truth they do have (8:18)?

b. What does 8:18 imply for your life?

77

For Thought and Discussion: Why do you think Jesus' power terrifies some people? Try to think about what happened to the Gerasenes from their point of view (8:32-37).

For Thought and Discussion: How should we respond when Jesus exhibits His power in our lives (Proverbs 9:10; Luke 5:8-11, 8:38-39)?

Legion (8:30). A Roman legion comprised six thousand soldiers.

Abyss (8:31). The pit where evil spirits and Satan will be confined when God's Kingdom is fulfilled (Revelation 9:1-6, 20:1-10).

Pigs (8:32). Pigs were unclean and forbidden food to Jews (Leviticus 11:7-8). Decapolis, however, was a largely Gentile region (see the map on page 11).

5. How did these three groups of people respond to Jesus when they saw His power in Gerasa and on the sea?

The disciples (8:25) _____

_____

_____

_____

The Gerasenes (8:34-37)_____

_____

_____

_____

The freed demoniac (8:38-39) _____

_____

_____

_____

A girl and a woman (8:40-56)

Crowds (8:42). Near-Eastern towns had narrow, winding streets that were always packed during the day. Haste in an emergency was nearly impossible in the face of street vendors, children, beggars, shoppers, and animals.

Bleeding (8:43). Like leprosy, bleeding made a person ceremonially unclean. For twelve years this woman had been barred from worship services, and even her friends would have avoided touching her.

6. Once again, Jesus revealed His power (8:40-56). What do you learn about Him as a person—His character and priorities—from this incident?

_____

_____

_____

_____

_____

_____

7. What would it take to keep trusting Jesus in the situation Jairus faced?

_____

_____

_____

_____

_____

_____

8. How would you summarize what the disciples might have learned from the events of 8:22-56?

_____

_____

_____

_____

_____

_____

For Thought and Discussion: What obstacles tempted Jairus to abandon hope of help (8:41-53)?

For Thought and Discussion:
a. Why do you think Jesus made the woman confront Him publicly (8:45-48)? What did the confrontation accomplish?
b. What did it reveal about Jesus' character and His aims?

Optional Application: Meditate on 8:39,48, or 50. Think about how Jesus' words apply to you.

For Thought and Discussion:
a. Why were preaching the Kingdom and healing the sick both parts of the Twelve's mission (9:2)? (Consider 4:18-19, 5:17-25.)

b. Why did Jesus command the Twelve to conduct their mission as in 9:3-5?

Optional Application:
In what general ways does the disciples' mission apply to Christians? In what specific ways does it apply to you? How can you act on your mission in the next few weeks?

The Twelve sent (9:1-9)

9. How was the mission of the Twelve related to Jesus' own mission? (Compare 7:22, 8:1, 9:2.)

_____

_____

_____

_____

Shake the dust off (9:5). Jews shook the dust of Gentile cities from their feet before returning to their land; Gentile dust would have defiled the ritually clean land of a holy people.[4]

Five thousand fed (9:10-17)

Having fulfilled their mission as Jesus' heralds, the Master takes the disciples across the lake alone to rest and reflect (Mark 6:31), but the crowds follow. Jesus postpones His students' rest for one more day to teach the crowds some important lessons. The feeding of the five thousand is the only miracle (other than the resurrection) recorded in all four Gospels.

10. What attitudes toward needy people does Jesus model for His disciples (9:11-13)?

_____

_____

_____

_____

11. The disciples had taken no provisions for food or shelter on their practice mission (9:3), but their needs had been met. What should the disciples have learned from their experience?

_____

_____

_____

_____

_____

12. How does the feeding of the five thousand reinforce the lesson the disciples should have learned (9:16-17)?

_____

_____

_____

_____

_____

13. Put yourself in the place of the disciples in 9:1-17. How are the lessons they learned also lessons you could apply?

_____

_____

_____

_____

_____

Who is Jesus? (9:18-27)

14. How does the disciples' understanding of Jesus exceed that of the crowds (9:18-20)?

_____

_____

_____

_____

_____

For Thought and Discussion: How do we know when to keep laboring for the Kingdom and when to pause for rest and reflection (9:10-11)? How do we deal with the seemingly endless needs of people around us?

For Further Study: See Psalm 23:1; Isaiah 25:6-9; Ezekiel 34:11-16,23-31 for lessons we can learn through the miracle of the loaves and fishes.

For Thought and Discussion: What impression has Jesus given so far about what it means to be the Christ? (Consider a few of these verses: 5:20,24,32; 6:5,20-22,46; 7:14,22,48; 8:24,28-32,44,53-56; 9:16-17.)

Warned them not to tell (9:21). "The people had false notions about the Messiah and needed to be taught further before Jesus identified himself explicitly to the public. He had a crucial schedule to keep and could not be interrupted by premature reactions."[5]

Son of Man (9:22). "Jesus' most common title for himself. . . . In Daniel 7:13-14 the Son of Man is pictured as a heavenly figure who in the end times is entrusted by God with authority, glory and sovereign power."[6] God calls Ezekiel "son of man" (Ezekiel 33:2), so the title also suggests that Jesus is a prophet, fully human, and a representative of humanity before God.

15. What new aspect of Christhood does Jesus want the disciples to understand (9:22)?

_____

_____

_____

_____

16. Recall 6:40. What does Jesus' mission (9:22) imply for His disciples (9:23-24)?

_____

_____

_____

_____

Take up his cross (9:23). Crucifixion was a common way in which the Romans executed slaves and lower class people. In the cities of Palestine, condemned men were frequently seen carrying heavy wooden crossbeams to the place of execution. The disciples knew that a man carrying a crossbeam was going to suffer and die.

17. Name one way in which a modern Christian may be tempted to "save his life" (9:24).

_____

_____

_____

_____

_____

_____

Optional Application: Think of one or two specific ways to deny yourself and take up your cross daily.

The Transfiguration (9:28-36)

Moses and Elijah (9:30). Both men had left the world in unusual ways, and both "were regarded as types of figures to appear at the end of the age."[7] The Law required two witnesses to certify the truth of anything (Deuteronomy 19:15); Moses the lawgiver represented the witness of the Law to Jesus, and Elijah represented the witness of the Prophets. Also, their presence proved that Jesus was neither Moses nor Elijah reborn, but greater than both, for He was going to fulfill both their ministries.

Cloud (9:34). The glory of the Lord appearing in the same form as when it descended on Mount Sinai, when Moses entered it to receive the Law of God (Exodus 24:15-18).

18. Explain the meaning of the Father's witness to Jesus (9:35). What was the Father trying to tell the disciples?

_____

_____

_____

_____

_____

For Thought and Discussion: A week earlier, Peter had identified Jesus as the Messiah. Jesus had tried to clarify what fulfilling that role would mean and what loyalty to such a Messiah would require. What did the disciples learn about the Messiah from this mountaintop experience?

For Thought and Discussion:
a. Why were Jesus' disciples unable to cast out the evil spirit (Luke 9:41, Mark 9:28-29)?
b. What do you make of that? Does it have any relevance to us today?

A deliverance and a perplexing promise
(9:37-45)

19. Jesus first predicted His rejection, execution, and resurrection after Peter acclaimed Him Christ (9:22). A week later He predicted His betrayal even while the people were marveling at His power over demons (9:43-44). What might Jesus have been trying to teach the disciples by timing His predictions alongside those events?

_____

_____

_____

_____

_____

An argument (9:46-50)

Having failed to understand Jesus' prediction of suffering and betrayal, and having been afraid to admit their obtuseness, the disciples begin to argue about the pecking order among them.

20. How did Jesus respond to this argument about who was the greatest (9:47-48)?

_____

_____

_____

_____

_____

21. How does the disciples' argument show yet again their misconceptions of Christhood and discipleship (9:20-26,44-45,48)?

_____

_____

84

_____

_____

_____

_____

_____

Samaritan opposition (9:51-56)

This scene continues the theme of the rest of chapter 9—correcting the disciples' mistaken notions. It also looks forward to more detailed instructions for ambassadors sent ahead of Jesus (10:1).

Samaritan (9:52). After King Solomon's death in 931 BC, his kingdom was split in two. The northern nation of Israel (with its capital at Samaria) rejected the southern nation of Judah (whose capital was at Jerusalem). The two nations remained bitter enemies until Assyria destroyed Israel in 723 BC. Assyria deported most Israelites and replaced them with conquered pagans from other countries.

From then on the region was always called Samaria, not Israel (2 Kings 17:24-29). Although some Samaritans continued to worship the Lord (2 Chronicles 34:6-10), most practiced a religion that combined elements of pagan religion with elements of biblical faith.

The Jews of Judah regarded the Samaritans as worse than Gentiles, while the Samaritans hated the Jews for rejecting them as well as for encroaching on their land. (Jews resettled formerly Samaritan territory in areas like Galilee.) Samaritans refused overnight shelter to Jews making the three-day pilgrimage from Galilee to Jerusalem for feast days, and Jews often traveled on the east side of the Jordan River to avoid Samaria.

Call fire down (9:54). Fire had consumed men who challenged Moses' leadership (Numbers 16:35). Elijah had called fire down upon soldiers sent to challenge his prophetic authority (2 Kings 1:9-16).

For Thought and Discussion: a. What might it mean to "welcome" (NASB: "receive") a child in Jesus' name (9:48)?
b. Why would welcoming a child in Jesus' name be equivalent to welcoming Jesus?

Optional Application: Have you ever wanted figuratively to call fire down on people who openly reject Jesus or you? What attitudes does this desire reflect? What attitudes would Jesus have you adopt? Ask Him to enable you to do this, and plan to memorize 6:27 and 9:54-55.

For Thought and Discussion: What implications does 9:58 have for the life of a modern disciple?

For Thought and Discussion: a. What is the first priority for a person who is spiritually alive (9:60)?
   b. What can this priority sometimes cost (9:59-60)?

22. James and John believed the Samaritans deserved to be destroyed by fire from heaven, but Jesus rebuked them (9:55). What lessons about Christhood and discipleship had they failed to learn (4:25-27, 6:27-38)?

_____

_____

_____

_____

_____

The cost of discipleship (9:57-62)

Bury my father (9:59). The duty of burial superseded even study of the Law, service in the Temple, killing the Passover sacrifice, or circumcision.[8] Not to bury a parent was "scandalous."[9] Thus, although the second man's request was reasonable, he may have wanted to wait until after his father's death, which may have been months or years away.[10]

---

23. What costs and risks of following Him does Jesus describe in 9:57-62?

_____

_____

_____

_____

_____

_____

24. What is the most personally relevant thing you have learned about discipleship from chapters 8–9?

_____

_____

_____

_____

_____

_____

25. What questions do you have from chapters 8–9?

_____

_____

_____

_____

_____

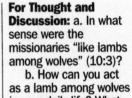

For Thought and Discussion: a. In what sense were the missionaries "like lambs among wolves" (10:3)?

b. How can you act as a lamb among wolves in your daily life? What are the dangers of doing this, and why is it necessary?

1. *The NIV Study Bible*, page 1553.
2. Morris, page 149.
3. *The NIV Study Bible*, page 1553.
4. Morris, page 164.
5. *The NIV Study Bible*, page 1557.
6. *The NIV Study Bible*, page 1510.
7. Marshall, page 380.
8. Morris, page 180.
9. Marshall, page 411.
10. *The NIV Study Bible*, page 1559.

Luke 10–11

With Great Authority

Everything Jesus did, He did with authority. He taught the people with authority, He commanded spiritual opponents with authority, and He dealt with His own disciples with authority. There should have been no doubt about who He claimed to be . . . and yet there was great doubt.

Read chapters 10–11, watching for the authoritative way Jesus deals with every one of the important matters that crosses His path.

The second mission (10:1-20)

On the road to Jerusalem, Jesus sent seventy-two[1] of His disciples to prepare His coming to the villages of Judea, just as He had sent the Twelve on a practice mission in Galilee.

1. What mission did Jesus give the seventy-two (10:1,2,9)?

_____

_____

_____

_____

_____

For Thought and Discussion: a. Why do you think the command "Ask the Lord . . ." (10:2) precedes the command "Go!" (10:3)?

b. How can you put both of these commands into practice?

Optional Application: The church has inherited a mission like that of the seventy-two (Matthew 28:18-20). Name at least one way in which you could use something in Luke 10:2-11 as a model for your own ministry.

For Further Study: Why were Korazin, Bethsaida, and Capernaum worthy of condemnation (10:13-15)? Luke 4:31-44, 5:17-26, and 7:1-10 describe Jesus' ministry in Capernaum.

Do not greet . . . do not move around (10:4,7). Eastern greetings could be long and elaborate,[2] and visiting a village could bog the missionaries down into social visits from house to house. By contrast, the greeting to the host was important to Jesus (10:5-6).

2. What might the disciples have learned about the priorities in their mission from the following instructions?

a. Do not take provisions (10:4)

b. Do not greet anyone or move around (10:4,7)

Tyre and Sidon (10:13). These had been Phoenician commercial centers. They had ignored the Lord's prophets and so had been judged (Isaiah 23, Ezekiel 26–28). By Jesus' time, Tyre and Sidon had been rebuilt. They were Gentile cities north of Galilee and had not witnessed the signs of the Kingdom that the towns of Galilee had seen.

3. Jesus reiterated that His disciples had His authority (10:16,19; compare 9:1). Why was it important to stress this?

_____

_____

_____

4. The disciples were joyful when Jesus' authority
   made them successful (10:17). But what should
   give a disciple even more joy (10:20), and why?

_____

_____

_____

_____

_____

Thanksgiving (10:21-24)

Jesus now offers a prayer of praise to God that should
overcome any related pride.

5. What "things" has the Father revealed to the disciples that set them apart from "the wise and learned"
   (10:21) and from "prophets and kings" (10:24)?

_____

_____

_____

_____

_____

6. According to 10:22, how is it possible to know God?

_____

_____

_____

_____

Optional Application:
Have you ever been
proud of what you know
about God? How does
10:21-24 affect your
inclination to be proud?

The lawyer's question (10:25-28)

How do you read it (10:26). A Jewish idiom that
   meant something like, "How do you recite?" That
   is, what law do you recite in daily worship? The
   obvious answer was the *Shema* (Deuteronomy 6:4-
   5). Since Matthew and Mark record similar encounters when Jesus named Deuteronomy 6:5 and
   Leviticus 19:18 as the greatest commandments
   (Matthew 22:34-40, Mark 12:28-34), this lawyer
   may well have been quoting Jesus' own teaching.[3]

7. According to Jesus, what should be a person's two
   priorities in life (10:27-28)?

_____

_____

_____

_____

_____

_____

_____

_____

Heart . . . soul . . . strength . . . mind (10:27). These
   were not meant to denote distinct parts of a per-
   sonality; Hebrew used parallelism for emphasis.
   The sense is to love with your whole being.[4]

8. Jesus said, "Do this and you will live" (10:28). What
   is the problem with trying to inherit eternal life in
   this way?

_____

_____

_____

_____

_____

The good Samaritan (10:29-37)

The expert in Scripture looked foolish when his attempt to test Jesus merely led to his agreeing with an orthodox doctrine that any schoolboy could have stated. Therefore, the expert asked what he thought was a tougher question.

_____

Neighbor (10:29). Jews understood a neighbor to be a member of one's religious community. Pharisees tended to exclude common people (lukewarm in their obedience to the Law), and other sects excluded anyone they considered to be Jews only in name. The lawyer tried to restore his dignity by asking Jesus whom He included in the community of people who deserved love.

Jerusalem to Jericho (10:30). This road ran through desolate, rocky wastes and descended 3,300 feet in its seventeen miles, so it was an ideal place for robbers.

Levite (10:32). A religious official below a priest but still privileged.

_____

9. The legal scholar asked, "Who is my neighbor?" — Whom must I love? What answer does the parable give?

_____

_____

_____

_____

Serving Jesus (10:38-42)

Luke 10:30-37 explains the second commandment: Love your neighbor. Now 10:38–11:13 explains the first commandment: Love God.

For Thought and Discussion: What does it mean to "love" God and "love" your neighbor?

For Thought and Discussion: What does 10:26-28 show about Jesus' attitude toward the Jewish Law?

For Thought and Discussion: What was wrong with the lawyer's notion of a neighbor?

Optional Application: Do you regard anyone as the expert regarded Samaritans? If so, ask God to change your heart. How can you practice love toward those people?

93

Optional Application:
How can you practice
Mary's choice this
week?

For Further Study:
"Father" (11:2) trans-
lates the Aramaic
address, Abba (see
2:49), which means
something like "Daddy."
What attitude toward the
Father does this address
imply?

Work (10:40). Literally, "serving."

10. What did Martha think it meant to serve Jesus
    (10:40)?

    _____

    _____

    _____

    _____

11. What service was more important to Him
    (10:41-42)?

    _____

    _____

    _____

12. How does this story further unfold Jesus' answer to
    how we can love God with our whole being?

    _____

    _____

    _____

Prayer (11:1-13)

Prayer is one of Luke's favorite themes. He shows Jesus
praying more often than the other Gospel writers do
and he includes more of Jesus' teaching on prayer.

Hallowed (11:2). To hallow is to treat as holy, to
  honor, to use with the utmost reverence.

Name (11:2). God's name represents His reputation,
  His person, His character.

94

13. What order of priorities does this prayer reveal (11:2-4)?

_____

_____

_____

_____

_____

_____

14. In 11:5-8, the audience is the disciples and the points of reference are the man in bed and the man outside. What is the point of this parable?

_____

_____

_____

_____

15. What is the message of the comparison in 11:11-13?

_____

_____

_____

_____

For Thought and Discussion: In what ways does your prayer tend to follow the priorities in 11:2-4, and in what ways does it differ?

For Thought and Discussion: Most of us know we fail to love the Samaritans and others around us, and that our prayers and time with Jesus are imperfect. What solution does Jesus offer for our weakness (11:4,13)?

Jesus versus Beelzebub (11:14-28)

Beelzebub (11:15). Or, "Beelzebul." Baal-Zebul was an honorific title for the Canaanite god: "Prince Baal" or "Exalted Baal." The Hebrews called him Baal-Zebub, meaning "lord of flies" (2 Kings 1:2). The name came to be used for the prince of demons.[5]

95

Optional Application:
Compare 9:49-50 and
11:23-26. How do these
verses apply to the way
you view others' work
and the way you view
your own?

For Further Study:
Other Jews were casting
out demons while
standing apart from the
rest of Jesus' mission
(11:19). In light of
11:24-26, do you think
those Jews were
"scattering" or
"gathering" (11:23)?
Why?

16. Some observers showed no doubt about the source of Jesus' power over demons. What was their verdict (11:15)?

_____

_____

_____

17. Others were unsure. How did they deal with the uncertainty (11:16)?

_____

_____

_____

Your judges (11:19). There were Jews who attempted to cast out demons.[6] Since any success they enjoyed must have been by God's power, to accuse Jesus of Satanic power was to accuse these other exorcists as well.

---

18. How can a witness be sure that Jesus works by God's Spirit and heralds God's Kingdom, not Satan's (11:17-20)?

_____

_____

_____

_____

With me . . . against me (11:23). Luke 9:50 and 11:23 appear to contradict each other. But notice that in 9:49-50 Jesus says that someone exorcising *in Jesus' name* should be regarded as being on the disciples' side (unless he opposes them). By contrast, in 11:23 He is talking about who is *with me*, not *with you* (9:50).

---

19. Every person is either helping Jesus to heal and save or hindering Him. In light of 11:20,24-26, describe . . .

a. How to gather with Jesus:

_____

_____

_____

_____

b. How to scatter against Him:

_____

_____

_____

_____

For Thought and Discussion: To call a person's mother blessed was a pious way of praising him. Of course, Mary was blessed (1:48), but what would have been a better response to Jesus' teaching (11:28)?

For Thought and Discussion: a. Why do you suppose miraculous signs like Jesus' and Jonah's often fail to convince skeptics?
b. What kinds of signs to prove the gospel's truth do people of your generation ask for? Why do you think they want those signs?

The sign of Jonah (11:29-32)

Jonah (11:29). This prophet spent three days in the belly of a fish until God miraculously "resurrected" him and sent him to proclaim God's words to the Assyrian capital, Nineveh. Both the Ninevites and the Queen of the South (1 Kings 10:1-13) were Gentiles—heathens in the eyes of Jesus' audience. If Ninevites repented after hearing Jonah and the queen of Sheba responded after hearing Solomon, then the Jews should certainly have repented after hearing Jesus.

20. Why was it wicked to ask Jesus for a sign to prove that He was from God (11:14,16,29-32)?

_____

_____

_____

97

For Further Study:
    a. How is it possible
to obtain good spiritual
eyes (10:21-24,
11:9-13)?
    b. What choices lead
a person into or out of
spiritual blindness
(8:4-15)?

The lamps (11:33-36)

Jesus again compares the message of the Kingdom to light, but here He is talking about His audience's perceptivity. Jesus has been openly preaching the message and performing signs by the Spirit of God (the light is shining all around) but His audience has failed to perceive it (11:14-32).[7]

Good (11:34, RSV). "Sound"; Greek: "single." That is, focused, singleminded.[8]

---

21. What does 11:33 say about the availability of the gospel to Jesus' hearers?

22. Why do some people fail to see the light of God's Kingdom (11:34)?

23. What should a person do to enable Jesus' message to enlighten his soul (11:34-36)?

Six woes (11:37-54)

Wash (11:38). Pharisees rinsed their hands before meals to remove the defilement of a sinful world, not physical dirt. The Scriptures did not require this.

Clean the outside (11:39). The Pharisees did clean both the inside and outside of dishes, as Jewish law required. Jesus was referring to ritual washings of the body, which the Pharisees required for all kinds of situations.

Unmarked graves (11:44). Contact with a grave made a Jew unclean, so graves were painted white to warn people. An unmarked grave defiled the person who walked on it unaware.

Optional Application: Meditate on 11:39-44. Ask God to enable you to give from the heart (11:41), devote yourself to justice and love (11:42), or grow less enamored of status and popularity (11:43). Ask God whether you can do anything actively to live out this transformation.

24. How were the Pharisees like dishes washed only on the outside (11:39) and graves that look like ordinary ground (11:39,42-44)?

_____

_____

_____

_____

Load people down (11:46). The scribes expanded the Law of Moses with rules that they thought clarified and protected the Law. But the experts who knew all the technicalities managed to obey by maneuvering through loopholes, which the common people knew nothing about.

Abel . . . Zechariah (11:51). Abel was the first man ever murdered, killed by his brother (Genesis 4:8). The murder of Zechariah is recorded in 2 Chronicles 24:20-22, in the last book of the Old Testament according to the Hebrew order.

25. Describe one way in which a modern person could have a fault like that of the Pharisees and teachers (11:39-44,46-52).

_____

_____

_____

_____

99

Optional Application:
a. Do any needs within or outside your group offer you chances to practice the neighbor relationship?
b. How can you practice the relationship toward God that 10:38–11:13 describes? How might this teaching affect your worship and prayer in your group?

26. Jesus denounced the Pharisees for being clean on the outside but filthy inside. How does a person become clean inside (11:13,24-26,40-41,42)?

_____

_____

_____

_____

_____

27. What insight from chapters 10–11 seems most significant to you personally right now?

_____

_____

_____

_____

28. What questions do you have on Luke 10–11?

_____

_____

_____

_____

1. Many good manuscripts say "seventy." See the full explanation in Marshall, pages 414-415.
2. Marshall, page 418.
3. Marshall, pages 442-444.
4. Marshall, pages 443-444.
5. *The NIV Study Bible*, page 1457.
6. Luke 9:49; Acts 19:13-14; Josephus *Antiquities* 8:45-48; and the Talmud all mention Jewish exorcists. Josephus and the Talmud describe successful exorcisms. See Marshall, page 474; H.L. Strack and P. Billerbeck, *Kommentar zum Neuen Testament aus Talmud und Midrasch* (Munich, 1956), volume 3, section 1, pages 527-535.
7. Marshall, pages 487-488.
8. Morris, page 202.

Luke 12:1–13:17

On the Alert

Jesus is preparing His disciples to face the crisis that will come after His death, but He is also urging the Jews to prepare for the disaster that even now looms on the horizon.

In a year Jesus will be gone from the earth; then His disciples will have to build the church by the Holy Spirit's guidance. In AD 70, less than forty years later, the Jews will rebel against Rome and the Roman army will crush Jerusalem and massacre its people. Yet Jesus tells His disciples not to fear people, even if those people have the power to put them to death. Rather, the disciples should fear God, who has the power to destroy or protect the whole person.

Fearless confession (12:1-12)

Having thoroughly rebuked the religious experts, Jesus left the Pharisee's home (11:53). If the religious men were not already set against Jesus, this incident made them His sworn enemies (11:53-54). Still, the crowds continue to acclaim Him (12:1). But regardless of enemies and admirers, Jesus' first concern was to instruct His disciples.

Hypocrisy (12:1). The Greek word *hypokritos* means "actor," a man who wears a mask and plays a role in the theater.

101

1. Why is hypocrisy dangerously foolish (12:1-3)?

_____

_____

_____

_____

_____

2. What fear can motivate a hypocrite to act as other people want him to act (12:4)?

_____

_____

_____

_____

_____

3. What fear should prevent hypocrisy (12:5)?

_____

_____

_____

_____

4. What certain knowledge should encourage a person to be fearlessly open about his or her true beliefs and character (12:6-7)?

_____

_____

_____

_____

_____

Blasphemes against the Holy Spirit (12:10). When the Holy Spirit reveals to someone that Jesus is the Savior, the Lord, and the Son of God, that person has two choices. He can *acknowledge* Jesus as his own Lord and Savior and become a disciple (12:8), or he can *disown* Jesus and try to remain his own master (12:9). To disown Jesus when the Holy Spirit has revealed Him is to blaspheme against the Holy Spirit. It is impossible for God to forgive a person who knowingly refuses to repent and be forgiven. By contrast, God can forgive a person who merely *speaks against* Jesus before He knows that Jesus is truly the Son of God.[1]

For Thought and Discussion: How is hypocrisy like yeast (12:1)?

For Thought and Discussion: In light of 1 John 4:18, why is it right that we fear God? Consider Luke 12:5, 35-48 and Proverbs 1:7.

For Thought and Discussion: Talk honestly about your fears of acknowledging Jesus openly. What are you afraid of?

Optional Application: a. What keeps you from being fully open about your faith in Jesus? Embarrassment? Concern for others' opinions? Fear of driving people further from Jesus? Respect for their beliefs?
   b. How can you be open without being pushy? See 1 Peter 3:14-16.

5. Why does Jesus refuse to accept secret disciples who will not acknowledge Him in public (12:8-10)? See also 8:16-18, 24:48.

_____

_____

_____

_____

6. How does God equip disciples to acknowledge Jesus when it is risky to do so (12:11-12)?

_____

_____

_____

_____

The rich fool (12:13-21)

As Jesus is teaching His disciples, an angry man pushes through the crowd to demand that Jesus perform one of the functions that rabbis often performed: arbitration in a dispute over a will.

For Thought and Discussion: According to 12:13-21, what should and shouldn't we be afraid of?

For Thought and Discussion: What message does 12:15-21 offer to a man who thinks he has been cheated? To a person who has abundant material goods? To you?

Arbiter (12:14). Literally, "divider." Compare 12:51,57.

Self . . . life (12:19,20,23). Or, "soul" (KJV). The Greek word *psyche* means "self," "soul," and "life" in the sense of an individual's life. Aramaic and Hebrew also have one word that means both soul and life.

---

7. Jesus refuses to judge or divide between two greedy sons (12:14). Instead, He tells a parable to show how God will judge all men like these (12:15-21). What is the rich man's mistake?

_____

_____

_____

_____

_____

Anxiety (12:22-34)

Jesus' disciples were not rich men; they were burdened by Roman and Jewish taxes, and they could barely manage peasant lifestyles. But as the man of 12:13 showed, the poor and middle class are as likely as the rich to be wrapped up in material things. Therefore, Jesus went on to teach His disciples some more on this subject.

8. How is worry related to greed? (Compare 12:15 with 12:22-34.)

_____

_____

_____

_____

_____

9. Why is worry unnecessary? List as many reasons as you can find in 12:22-34.

_____

_____

_____

_____

_____

_____

_____

_____

For Thought and Discussion: How does worry dishonor God?

Optional Application:
    a. The command in 12:33 can be shocking. How might it apply to you?
    b. Take time daily this week to talk to the Father about 12:33. How can you apply this severe command?

10. What does it mean to seek the Kingdom that God has given us (12:31)? Write down at least one specific way you can seek the Kingdom.

_____

_____

_____

_____

_____

_____

11. In 12:32 Jesus again says, "Do not be afraid." What should we not be afraid of?

_____

_____

_____

_____

Optional Application:
Meditate on the last part
of 12:48, and consider
what material goods,
abilities, knowledge, and
responsibilities you have
been given. How can
you use these to store
up treasures in heaven?

Readiness (12:35-48)

Instead of worrying about his livelihood, a disciple
should focus his hopes, fears, and energy elsewhere.

Be dressed ready for service (12:35). Literally, "let
  your loins be girded" (NASB margin). A man work-
  ing hard, fighting, etc., lifted the hem of his flowing garment and tied it into his belt for freedom of
  movement.

Keep your lamps burning (12:35). Only someone stay-
  ing awake all night to watch or work would do this.

Second or third watch (12:38). The Jews divided the
  night into three watches. A banquet (12:36) would
  have begun with the first watch, at sunset. The
  second watch went from 10 p.m. to 2 a.m., and
  the third was from 2 a.m. to dawn (Judges 7:19).[2]

---

12. According to 12:35-40, what should a wise disciple
    do, and why?

    _____

    _____

    _____

    _____

    _____

    _____

13. What will happen at Christ's return to His servants
    who:

    a. justly discharge their responsibilities to servants
       under their charge (12:42-44)?

    _____

    _____

    _____

    _____

106

b. abuse their authority over others (12:45-46)?

_____

_____

_____

_____

For Thought and Discussion: Why does Jesus' divisiveness not contradict His mission as the bringer of peace (2:14)?

c. fail to do Jesus' will out of laziness or preoccupation with personal goals (12:47)?

_____

_____

_____

_____

d. fail to do Jesus' will out of ignorance (12:48)?

_____

_____

_____

_____

Division (12:49-53)

Fire (12:49). Judgment is a fire that consumes the wicked and leaves the righteous, a fire that separates the dross from pure metal (3:16-17). Jesus was going to suffer the fire of God's judgment for humanity on the cross.

Baptism (12:50). Jesus' death was like a baptism—a drowning deluge of judgment for our sin.

For Thought and Discussion: a. Jesus said He did not come to impose a just redistribution of material goods among equally selfish people (12:13-15). But what did He say to people who use their goods selfishly (12:15-21)? How did He advise His disciples to use their goods (12:32-34, 14:12-14, 16:9-12)?

b. What recourse does this leave to the poor and oppressed in this life (12:22-32, 18:1-8)?

Optional Application: Consider memorizing and meditating on a verse or passage from this lesson that especially challenges or encourages you. Prayerfully make a list of all the implications that text has for you. Then act on and pray diligently about one of those implications.

Division (12:51). Luke 12:52-53 follows Micah 7:6 in predicting division between generations in a family: father and mother against daughter, son, and son's wife.

14. Jesus said He did not come to divide men's material goods (12:13-15). What did He come to divide (12:42-48,51-53)?

_____

_____

_____

_____

_____

Discernment (12:54-59)

West . . . south (12:54-55). Wind from the west brought moisture from the Mediterranean, while wind from the south brought dry heat from the desert. The people cared enough about the weather to watch for signs to predict it, but they failed to notice signs of approaching moral disaster.

15. a. Why do people care enough about the weather to predict and prepare for it?

_____

_____

_____

_____

b. Why do people fail to foresee and prepare for their own judgment?

_____

_____

_____

_____

Judge for yourselves (12:57). The common people of
Jesus' day tended to rely on their leaders—priests,
Pharisees, teachers of Scripture, heads of fami-
lies—to tell them what God expected.

---

16. Jesus presents us with two alternatives in light of
approaching judgment (12:57-59).

a. How can we be reconciled to our adversary, God
(12:57-58)?

_____

_____

_____

_____

_____

b. What is the alternative (12:58-59)?

_____

_____

_____

_____

_____

Repentance (13:1-9)

Jesus' talk of judgment led some men to describe a
dreadful punishment certain Galileans had suffered.

Pilate (13:1). The governor of Judea, who figures later
in Jesus' story. Non-biblical sources also testify to
his rash cruelty.

17. The Jews looked at tragedies and concluded that the victims must have deserved it. But what lesson should the people have learned from the sudden deaths (13:1-5)?

_____

_____

_____

_____

_____

Fig tree (13:6). A common symbol of the Jewish nation. Still, the parable applies equally to individuals.

18. What does 13:6-9 tell us about:

a. God's character?

_____

_____

_____

b. Jesus' mission?

_____

_____

_____

c. The response God expects of His people?

_____

_____

_____

A Sabbath cure (13:10-17)

Luke inserted this story after the parable of the fig tree to show how the tree of Israel was responding to its last chance before being cut down.[3]

19. Hypocrisy was a recurring theme in Jesus' words for His people (12:1,56; 13:15). How did the synagogue ruler and others show hypocrisy in their attitude toward people, animals, Jesus, and the Sabbath (13:10-16)?

_____

_____

_____

_____

20. What currently seems to be the most important implication of 12:1–13:17 for your life? Review any applications you have already written, and choose one of those or another to focus on during the coming week.

_____

_____

_____

_____

21. List any questions you have about 12:1–13:17.

_____

_____

_____

_____

1. Wilcock, pages 131-132; Marshall, pages 516-519.
2. _The NIV Study Bible_, pages 1463, 1565.
3. Wilcock, page 139.

Optional Application:
Do you ever use God's commands to avoid actively loving your neighbor (13:14-16)? Ask God to show you if you do this.

Luke 13:18–16:18

Parables and Teachings

Luke includes more of Jesus' parables than any other Gospel, and in this section of his work he tells more parables than anywhere else. The Savior used parables to explain to His followers what it means to have faith, how to enter the Kingdom of God, and many other crucial lessons.

As crucial as Jesus' parables are, His other teachings are equally important, not only for what He says but for the commandingly authoritative way in which He presents them. But still the Pharisees and other religious leaders firmly reject Him.

As you read Luke 13:18–16:18, watch for the common themes that resurface again and again.

Kingdom parables (13:18-21)

Mustard seed (13:19). "It was the smallest seed used by Palestinian farmers," yet "the plant could reach some ten feet in height."[1]

Yeast (13:21). "In the Bible, yeast usually symbolizes that which is evil or unclean. . . . Here, however, it is a symbol of growth."[2]

1. How is the Kingdom of God like:

   a. A mustard seed (13:18-19)?

   _____

   _____

113

For Thought and Discussion: a. How are Jesus' healings and parables of the Kingdom signs of hope for some people and signs of warning for others (13:17)?

b. How should we respond to the parables of the mustard seed and the yeast?

For Thought and Discussion: On what basis will some people try to enter the Kingdom after it is too late (13:26)? Explain in your own words what Jesus is getting at.

For Further Study: What does 13:31-35 reveal about Jesus' mission and character?

b. Yeast (13:20-21)?

The narrow door (13:22-30)

As Jesus travels and teaches, someone asks Him about the number of people who will be saved (13:23). Instead of talking about "people" in general, Jesus replies with direct advice for the inquirer (13:24).

2. In what sense is the door to the Kingdom wide (13:18-19,28-30)?

3. In what sense is the door narrow (13:25,27)?

Prophets die in Jerusalem (13:31-35)

Fox (13:32). In Jewish thought, the fox was considered cunning but base.[3] Herod was widely despised as weak and treacherous.

114

Today and tomorrow (13:33). A Jewish idiom meaning "an uncertain, but limited period."[4]

House is left . . . desolate (13:35). Jesus foresaw that
God was going to abandon His city and Temple to
be destroyed by Rome. The magnificent Temple in
Jerusalem was utterly demolished in AD 70 and
has never been rebuilt.

Optional Application:
Tell someone the
message of
12:54–13:35. Or, work
on building a relationship
with someone so that
you can tell him or her
soon.

4. God gave His people a last chance (13:6-9), but
they ignored His warnings (12:54-59; 13:1-9,24-30)
and rejected His signs (13:10-17). How did Jesus
feel about His rebel people (13:34-35)?

_____

_____

_____

_____

Another Sabbath healing (14:1-6)

Dropsy (14:2). "An accumulation of fluid that would
indicate illness affecting other parts of the body."[5]
The Greek word is a technical medical term, more
evidence that a physician wrote this Gospel.

5. The religious men were willing to set aside their
rules about Sabbath work for the sake of one of
their sons or animals (14:5). If they would do this
and disallow the healing of strangers, what was
wrong with their priorities?

_____

_____

_____

_____

For Thought and Discussion: Why does the Kingdom of God operate on the principle of 14:11?

Optional Application: Try doing what 14:12-14 says. Or, get involved in serving the poor in some other way.

For Thought and Discussion: a. What kinds of excuses have you heard from people who are trying to evade God's invitation?
   b. Why would anyone want to evade an invitation to God's feast?

Banquet manners (14:7-14)

Places of honor (14:7). The seat at a host's right was the place of highest honor, then the host's left, and so on.

6. Luke 14:7-11 is probably not meant as advice for how to seek worldly status more cleverly. What do you think is Jesus' point in that passage?

_____

_____

_____

_____

_____

7. Why is it better to give hospitality to the poor and handicapped than to your friends and relatives (14:12-14)?

_____

_____

_____

_____

_____

The great banquet (14:15-24)

A pious remark (14:15) gives Jesus a chance to tell a parable about those who will and won't be among the blessed at the feast in the Kingdom. Jesus' audience is a group of Pharisees—busy, prosperous, respectable, religious men.

Feast in the kingdom (14:15). Isaiah had described God's Kingdom as a banquet (Isaiah 25:6), and the idea was common in Jesus' day (Luke 13:29, Revelation 19:9).

116

Sent his servant (14:17). In a world without clocks, it was customary to invite guests ahead of time and then send for them when the banquet was actually ready.

8. What is the point of the parable in 14:16-24? What response does it call for us to make?

_____

_____

_____

_____

_____

Study Skill: Hyperbole
Hyperbole is extreme exaggeration to make a point; it was a common Hebrew form of expression. In 14:12-14, Jesus doesn't mean we should *never* invite friends and relatives, but rather we should make a point of inviting the poor and needy. Likewise, in 14:26, "hate" means that we should love family and self so much less than Jesus that our love for them is like hatred compared to our love for Him. In Jesus' day, commitment to family was as intense as commitment to one's own life.

---

9. In 14:25-35, Jesus addresses the crowds who want to travel with Him (14:25). What does He tell those crowds to do in the two parables of 14:28-33?

_____

_____

_____

_____

_____

Salt (14:34). It was indispensable as a preservative, a flavoring, and an ingredient for holy sacrifice. Pure sodium chloride cannot lose its flavor, but the salt taken from the Dead Sea was mixed with carnal-lite. If the sodium chloride was dissolved away, the remainder was bitter.[6]

10. Jesus has been talking about the cost of disciple-ship. How is a would-be disciple who decides he cannot bear the cost, like salt that loses it saltiness (14:34-35)?

_____

_____

_____

_____

_____

11. Go back through 14:1-35 and write down each cost of discipleship that Jesus names.

_____

_____

_____

_____

_____

_____

_____

Sheep and coin (15:3-10)

12. According to the parables of the sheep and coin (15:3-10), how does God respond when one of His valued creatures or treasures is lost (15:4,8)?

_____

_____

_____

_____

_____

_____

13. What does God do and how does He feel when He finds His lost one (15:5-7,9-10)?

_____

_____

_____

_____

_____

_____

The lost son (15:11-32)

Share of the estate (15:12). A Jewish father sometimes divided his estate among his sons but continued to use the income from the whole estate until his death. It was extraordinary for a son to request his share along with its income before his father's death; it was equivalent to wishing the father's death.[7]

Pigs (15:15). Eating pigs was forbidden to Jews (Deuteronomy 14:8), and feeding them was unclean and "thoroughly degrading."[8]

Ran (15:20). The head of a family normally lived in the center of the village, rather than on the edge. Therefore, such a father could have seen his son a long way off only if he were intentionally watching for the young man from the roof of his house or from the village gate. It was considered extremely undignified and humiliating for a man to run, especially to greet someone. A man signified his own importance by waiting or at most walking to receive someone.

For Thought and Discussion: What complaint prompted Jesus to tell the three parables in chapter 15? How does this help you understand the message of the parables?

Optional Application: How can you share in heaven's joy over repentant sinners?

For Thought and Discussion: a. How is every person's decision to sin like the younger son's choices in 15:11-13?
    b. How is 15:17-21 a picture of any person's repentance?

For Thought and Discussion: How do the younger son's attitudes toward himself and his father change after he repents?

Optional Application: Do you identify more with the older or the younger son? Why?

14. In the first two parables, the shepherd and the
    woman with the lamp hunt diligently for their lost
    valuables. In the third parable, what brings the son
    to repentance (15:14-17)?

    _____

    _____

    _____

    _____

Robe . . . ring . . . sandals . . . feast (15:22-23). The
    quality of his robe showed a person's status, so the
    best robe went to the heir with the most authority.
    The ring was also a sign of authority. Shoes signi-
    fied that a man was a freeman and a master of the
    house, for slaves went barefoot and guests
    removed their shoes upon arrival. Meat was eaten
    only rarely, on special occasions; a fatted calf was
    saved for the most important events.[9]

15. How does the father treat the son who insulted him
    and squandered his wealth (15:20-24)?

    _____

    _____

    _____

    _____

16. How does the older son feel about his father's
    response to his brother? Why does he feel that way
    (15:25-30)?

    _____

    _____

    _____

    _____

    _____

17. What response does this parable ask from:

a. Sinners?

_____

_____

_____

_____

b. Pharisees?

_____

_____

_____

_____

c. You?

_____

_____

_____

_____

For Thought and Discussion: How do you think knowing that God is like the father in 15:11-32 should affect the way a Christian treats God, himself, and others?

The shrewd manager (16:1-9)

Manager (16:1). This steward (NASB, RSV) was in charge of his master's business affairs.

18. How is the manager's predicament (16:1-3) a picture of every sinner's predicament?

_____

_____

_____

_____

121

19. The manager doesn't throw himself on his master's mercy as the son does in 15:17-21. What does the manager do instead about his problem (16:4-7)?

_____

_____

_____

_____

_____

Called in each one (16:5). The manager's act may be interpreted in two ways. He may have crowned a dishonest career with extreme dishonesty, cheating his master of interest due him. Or, Jesus may have had the law of interest in mind. God's Law forbade men to charge interest on loans (Exodus 22:25-27), but men evaded that rule by lending oil or grain rather than money. The steward may have reduced the debts by the amount of interest charged (100 percent on oil was not unheard of). That interest may even have been his own commission on the loan, in which case he was truly spending his own wealth for later security.[10]

Worldly wealth (16:9). Literally, "mammon of unrighteousness." "Mammon" is an Aramaic word for wealth or possessions.

20. Jesus commends the manager's solution for one reason: the manager used money to win friends for himself in the world to which he was committed (16:8-9). What, then, is the lesson in this parable for us?

_____

_____

_____

_____

_____

122

Faithful stewardship (16:10-13)

21. In 16:10-13, Jesus commends a particular character trait of a good disciple: faithful or trustworthy stewardship. Why should you be faithful with whatever you have in this world?

16:10 _____

_____

_____

16:11 _____

_____

_____

16:12 _____

_____

_____

16:13 _____

_____

_____

Optional Application:
How can you use your Master's property more shrewdly to gain eternal friends (16:9) or more faithfully and honestly to gain true riches of your own (16:11)? Plan at least one specific application of 16:1-13.

The Pharisees reproved (16:14-18)

Justify yourselves (16:15). The Pharisees justified themselves in the eyes of men by giving alms liberally. However, they were proud and jealous of the ninety percent of their income which they kept, and they were always looking for ways to make more money. Therefore, Jesus did not consider their giving to be the faithful stewardship He commanded in 16:10-13.

For Thought and Discussion: What did the Pharisees value (esteem, exalt) that God detests (16:14-15)?

For Further Study: Luke 16:18 is an example of one of God's permanent laws of society. For more on this topic, see Matthew 5:31-32, 19:9; 1 Corinthians 7:10-11. See also Genesis 2:18-24 and Ephesians 5:21-33 on the marriage relationship; Luke 17:3-4 and John 8:1-11 on Jesus' attitude toward sinners and those who condemn them.

22. The Pharisees claimed to be justified by obeying every bit of the Law (16:15), but what part of the Law were they breaking (Deuteronomy 5:7,19,21; see Luke 16:14)?

_____

_____

_____

_____

23. What parable or teaching in 13:18–16:18 most grabs your attention? Why?

_____

_____

_____

_____

_____

_____

24. List your questions from 13:18–16:18.

_____

_____

_____

_____

1. *The NIV Study Bible*, page 1461.
2. *The NIV Study Bible*, page 1462.
3. Marshall, page 571.
4. Marshall, pages 571-572.
5. *The NIV Study Bible*, page 1568.
6. Marshall, page 596.
7. Marshall, page 607; *The NIV Study Bible*, page 1569.
8. Marshall, page 608.
9. Marshall, pages 610-611.
10. Marshall, pages 614-617.

Luke 16:19–18:34

The Way to Life

Jesus has been speaking alternately to His disciples and to the Pharisees about preparing now for the next world. The Father's joy at repentance and generous offer of the Kingdom is wonderful good news, but the Law still applies in all its rigor to those who reject the offer. Faithful stewardship of possessions, care for a brother, forgiveness, faith, and humility are all part of life in the Kingdom.

In 17:20-37, Jesus again speaks alternately to the Pharisees and the disciples about the coming Kingdom; in 18:1-14 He addresses to each group a different parable on prayer. In 17:11-19 Luke inserts an incident that vividly illustrates the contrast between two responses to Jesus. Read 16:19–18:34.

The rich man and Lazarus (16:19-31)

Jesus directs this parable to the Pharisees, who are not using their money in a godly way.

Abraham's side (16:22). In Jewish tradition, Abraham's "bosom" (KJV) is the home of the righteous, "the place of blessedness to which the righteous dead go to await future vindication."[1]

Hell (16:23). *Hades* is the Greek name for the underworld. The Jews had adopted this name for the place where the wicked dead go before the final judgment.[2] Some people consider this a literal

125

For Thought and Discussion: How should the Pharisees and lovers of money respond to this parable?

Optional Application: Ask God to impress upon you the urgency of 16:19-31 in your life. Ask Him to show you ways to act upon the parable this week.

For Thought and Discussion: Why do you think Jesus is so hard on a person who tempts another to sin (17:1-2)?

description of the afterlife before judgment, while others think Jesus is telling a parable with terms and ideas familiar to His hearers.

1. How could the rich man in 16:19-31 have attained the blessings Lazarus received (16:9,29,31)?

2. Why was the rich man's request in 16:27-28,30 futile?

Sin and faith (17:1-10)

Jesus has taught His disciples and rebuked the Pharisees about the use of worldly goods for the Kingdom. Along the same lines, Jesus now teaches His disciples more about how sons should behave once they have been welcomed back to their Father's estate (15:21-23).

Things that cause people to sin (17:1). "Stumbling blocks" in NASB. A person chooses his own sin, but someone who tempts or pressures him bears some responsibility.

3. What does Jesus say about a person who encourages another to sin (17:1-2)?

Seven times (17:4). The number seven signified full-ness. Compare Matthew 18:21-22.

4. Why does Jesus command the following two responses to a sinner (17:3-4)?

a. Rebuke (Matthew 18:15-17, 2 Corinthians 7:8-11)

_____

_____

_____

_____

_____

b. Continual forgiveness of the penitent (Matthew 18:15-35, Luke 6:36-42)

_____

_____

_____

_____

_____

5. What is Jesus' point about faith in Luke 17:5-6?

_____

_____

_____

_____

For Thought and Discussion: Why is it often hard to obey Luke 17:4? What can a Christian do about this difficulty?

Optional Application: Meditate on 17:3-4 or 17:6, and look for at least one way to apply that teaching actively this week.

For Thought and Discussion: How is 17:11-19 a lesson for us about discipleship?

6. How should God's servant feel even if he manages to exercise his faith to do everything God expects (17:7-10)?

_____

_____

_____

_____

The grateful Samaritan (17:11-19)

Samaritan (17:16). Leprosy put Jewish and foreign people on the same level; all were unclean and outcast so they associated together freely.

7. All ten lepers had enough faith in Jesus to ask for healing (17:12-13) and obey Him before they had proof of healing (17:14). What was unique about the Samaritan's response to Jesus (17:15-16)?

_____

_____

_____

_____

The coming of the Kingdom (17:20-37)

When the kingdom of God would come (17:20). The question probably requests an answer of the form: "The kingdom will come when you see so-and-so taking place."[3] Jesus replies that to look for signs is to misunderstand the Kingdom.

Within (17:21). Or, "among." Because Jesus always spoke of people entering the Kingdom, never the Kingdom entering people, some scholars think Jesus meant that signs were unnecessary because the Kingdom was already present in the midst of His hearers.[4] On the other hand, Jesus may have

128

meant that signs were unnecessary because the Kingdom is currently internal and invisible, not a physical invasion (John 18:36).

8. In what sense was the Kingdom already among Jesus' hearers (Luke 1:32-33, 4:18-21)?

_____

_____

_____

_____

_____

9. In what sense is the Kingdom of God (His sovereign rule, His presence, His blessings) *within* us individually, and in what sense is it *among* us corporately?

_____

_____

_____

_____

_____

10. Why were the Pharisees unable to perceive the Kingdom already among them or already available to be within them (see 11:34-36,39-44)?

_____

_____

_____

The days of the Son of Man (17:22). Probably the time of Christ's reign after His return.

For Thought and Discussion: Will a close relationship with a saved person guarantee a person's salvation (17:34-35)? Why, or why not?

11. a. What did Jesus say to do when people claim that the Son of Man has returned (17:22-25)?

_____

_____

_____

_____

b. What reasons did He give?

_____

_____

_____

_____

Lot's wife (17:32). While fleeing the destruction of sinful Sodom, she looked back with longing and so was turned into a pillar of salt (Genesis 18:16–19:26).

12. How will the days of the Son of Man be like the days of Noah and Lot (17:26-35)?

_____

_____

_____

_____

Body . . . vultures (17:37). Several interpretations have been suggested. Among them:

1. "Where?" means "Where will Jesus' return take place?" Jesus replies that just as vultures clearly indicate the presence of carrion, so plain evidence will clearly indicate Jesus' return (see Matthew 24:28).
2. "Where?" means "Where will the separation of 17:34-35 take place?" Jesus replies that wherever

"the spiritually dead are found, there inevitably will be judgment."[5] That is, the separation at Jesus' coming will happen everywhere.[6]

The unjust judge (18:1-8)

Jesus' return will be sudden and obvious, but it may not be soon. Therefore, Jesus teaches His disciples how to pray without knowing when the Son of Man will come.

13. The point of this parable grows out of a contrast between the judge and God.

 a. Why does the judge finally give justice to the widow (18:4-5)?

 _____

 _____

 _____

 b. How is God different from this judge (18:2,6-8)?

 _____

 _____

 _____

 _____

 c. How can disciples show "faith" (18:8) in God's character while they await Jesus' return (18:1,7)?

 _____

 _____

 _____

 _____

Two prayers (18:9-14)

To people like the Pharisees, Jesus tells a parable about the attitudes we should have as we pray.

131

For Thought and Discussion: What can we learn from 18:9-14 about how to relate rightly to God?

For Thought and Discussion: What wrong idea about the Kingdom do the disciples show by rebuking the babies' parents (18:15)?

Optional Application: How do you need to be more childlike toward God? Ask Him to help you become like this.

Justified (18:14). Accounted righteous in God's sight.

14. What is wrong with the Pharisee's attitude in prayer (18:11-12)?

_____

_____

_____

_____

15. What is good about the tax collector's attitude in prayer (18:13)?

_____

_____

_____

Jesus and children (18:15-17)

In this next section leading up to Jesus' royal ride into Jerusalem, the King makes a special point of clarifying the nature of His Kingdom.

16. In what ways must we be like children in order to be welcome in God's Kingdom (18:15-17)?

_____

_____

_____

_____

The rich ruler (18:18-30)

Ruler (18:18). A synagogue leader or a member of the *Sanhedrin*, the highest council of Jewish elders (see 22:66).[7]

Eternal life (18:18). The Gospels use three phrases that mean almost the same thing: eternal life (18:18,30); entering the Kingdom (18:17,25); and salvation (19:9-10).[8]

17. The ruler feels that he can confidently claim to have obeyed each of the commandments Jesus has named (18:21). But does Luke 18:22-23 suggest that the ruler is obeying the first commandment (Exodus 20:3) perfectly? Why or why not?

_____

_____

_____

18. a. What two things does Jesus say this man must do to be saved (18:22)?

_____

_____

_____

b. Why are these steps necessary for this particular man?

_____

_____

_____

19. Why is it hard for the rich to enter the Kingdom (18:24-25)?

_____

_____

_____

For Further Study: Jews sometimes described men as "good" (18:18), but rarely addressed them so. Why does Jesus challenge the man on his use of the word (18:19)?

For Thought and Discussion: Do you think anyone you know should sell his or her possessions and give them to the poor? Why do you think that?

133

Who then can be saved? (18:26). Jews thought prosperity signified God's favor, so no one was a better candidate for the Kingdom than a rich man.

20. What does Jesus promise to those who do decide to obey 14:33 and leave all for Him (18:29-30)?

_____

_____

_____

_____

21. What passage in 16:19–18:34 had the most impact on you? Explain.

_____

_____

_____

_____

_____

_____

22. List any questions you have about 16:19–18:34.

_____

_____

_____

_____

1. *The NIV Study Bible*, page 1572.
2. Marshall, pages 636-637; *The NIV Study Bible*, page 1572.
3. Marshall, pages 654-655.
4. Marshall, pages 655-656.
5. Morris, page 262.
6. Marshall, page 669.
7. Marshall, page 684.
8. *The NIV Study Bible*, page 1470.

Luke 18:35–19:44

The Son of David

In His final approach to Jerusalem, Jesus has attracted quite a crowd. Parents are bringing babies to be blessed by the prophet whom they believe to be the King of Israel. Jesus has been trying to teach His disciples that His Kingdom is for the poor, the childlike, those with nothing they will not gladly give up for the Kingdom of eternal life. Jesus has also repeatedly said that before the rewards of kingship will come rejection and death. But the disciples, and still worse the crowd, have grasped only the happy part of the message.

Hence, the last act is inevitable. As you read 18:35–19:44, observe closely what Jesus reveals about His kingship.

A blind man healed (18:35-43)

Son of David (18:38-39). A Messianic title. This descendant of David would reign forever as God's representative when God's Kingdom was fulfilled (2 Samuel 7:12-13, Psalm 89:3-4).

Mercy (18:38). As Jesus and His entourage approach Jerusalem, a blind beggar cries out to King David's royal Son for mercy. Luke's first readers would have recognized the familiar sight of a common man calling to a ruler for mercy as the ruler traveled through his territory. The ruler would summon the supplicant into his presence, hear the request, and perhaps grant it.[1]

Optional Application:
What request would you
like to bring before the
King (18:38-43)? Do so
now.

1. How does Jesus display His kingship and character
   in 18:35-43?

   _____

   _____

   _____

   _____

2. In what ways does the blind beggar show faith in
   the King (18:38-43)?

   _____

   _____

   _____

   _____

Zacchaeus the tax collector (19:1-10)

3. This story is included partly to illustrate Jesus'
   statement in 19:10. How does Jesus define His mission in that verse?

   _____

   _____

   _____

   _____

   _____

4. What does Jesus do to seek and save Zacchaeus
   (19:5)?

   _____

   _____

   _____

   _____

   _____

5. How does Zacchaeus show that he has truly embraced Jesus' offer of salvation (19:6,8)?

_____

_____

_____

_____

Sinner (19:7). As a chief tax collector, Zacchaeus was seen as an extortioner and collaborator by the crowd; he would have been unwelcome in Jewish homes and synagogues.

6. In what way does the crowd's muttering (19:7) show that they misunderstood Jesus' mission to the "poor" (4:18, 5:30-32, 6:20, 19:10)?

_____

_____

_____

_____

_____

Son of Abraham (19:9). A son of Abraham is a true Jew, a man whose faith and character are in Abraham's footsteps (see Romans 4:12).

The ten minas (19:11-27)

The audience of this parable is the disciples and the crowd, all of whom believed that the Kingdom of God would mean a political triumph over Israel's enemies.

7. What prompted Jesus to tell this parable (19:11)?

_____

_____

For Thought and Discussion: Short Zacchaeus must have looked foolish sitting in a tree and straining to see Jesus (19:4). In what way is his willingness to do this an example for us?

For Thought and Discussion: How does 19:8 show that Zacchaeus understands how Jesus' offer of friendship should affect his life?

For Thought and Discussion: How is 19:12 just like what Jesus did? How is 19:14 like what happened to Him?

For Further Study: Compare Luke 19:11-27 to Matthew 25:14-30.

Ten minas (19:13). One mina equaled one hundred drachmas, or about one hundred days' wages.

8. How does the returning king reward his servants who have multiplied their minas tenfold and five-fold (19:15-19)?

9. What mistaken belief about his master gets the third servant into trouble (19:20-23)?

10. What does the master do with the third servant's mina (19:24-26)?

11. What is the lesson for disciples in 19:13-26?

138

12. a. The unfruitful servant loses his mina, but what happens to the citizens who reject the king's rule entirely (19:14,27)?

For Thought and Discussion: How is the parable of 19:12-27 a response to the belief that the Kingdom is coming immediately (19:11)?

_____

_____

_____

_____

b. What point is Jesus making to the crowds in this part of the parable?

_____

_____

_____

_____

The triumphal entry (19:28-40)

Jesus entered Jerusalem on Sunday of the week Christians call Passion Week because it was the week of His suffering and death (Latin: *passio*).

Bethphage and Bethany (19:29). Two villages on the road between Jericho and Jerusalem. Not long before His final entry into Jerusalem, Jesus raised a man named Lazarus from the dead (John 11:1-44). The resurrection of Lazarus was still fresh in everyone's mind when Jesus rode into Jerusalem (John 12:12-19).

Colt (19:30). Pilgrims normally walked into Jerusalem, but a rabbi often rode while his disciples walked on foot.[2] An unbroken colt was ritually clean, suitable for sacred or royal use. Matthew 21:7 informs us that Jesus rode a donkey colt—a symbol of peace in contrast to a warrior's horse—to fulfill Zechariah 9:9.

The Lord (19:31). Jews normally reserved this title for God, but here Jesus is probably claiming the title for Himself. He has indeed come "in the name of the Lord" (19:38).

13. Read Zechariah 9:9-13. What was Jesus proclaiming about Himself by the way He entered Jerusalem (19:35-36)?

_____

_____

_____

_____

Blessed ... Lord (19:38). The disciples welcomed Jesus in the words of Psalm 118:26, which probably depicts a procession to the Temple in celebration of a king's victory. The Jews may have expected that the Messiah would enter the Temple speaking Psalm 118:5-21, then the people would respond with 118:22-29, and the Messiah would grasp the horns of the altar (118:27) and so declare Himself King. John 12:13 indicates that the crowd may have joined in shouting "Hosanna" ("O LORD, save us," Psalm 118:25), hoping that Jesus was indeed the liberator.

14. How did the Pharisees feel about the crowd treating Jesus like the Messiah (19:39)?

_____

_____

_____

_____

15. How did Jesus respond to being acclaimed Messiah (19:40)?

_____

_____

_____

_____

Lament over Jerusalem (12:41-44)

The Mount of Olives reaches about 2700 feet above sea level, some 300 feet above Jerusalem. The road from Jericho climbs steeply toward Bethany and the Mount, and then descends to Jerusalem.[3] While His disciples welcomed Him as the Messiah and the Pharisees rebuked Him, Jesus rounded the peak and began the ride down to the city. His first sight of it seems to have reminded Him that in just forty years Rome would besiege and destroy Jerusalem.

For Thought and Discussion: How did Jesus feel about Jerusalem's well-deserved destruction (19:41)?

16. a. What was hidden from Jerusalem's people that would have brought them "peace" (19:42)?

_____

_____

_____

_____

_____

b. How would it have brought them peace?

_____

_____

_____

_____

17. Meditate for a few minutes on the character Jesus reveals in 18:35-43 and 19:28-44, and on the destiny of the people who rejected their King (19:27,42-44). Does any of this move you to respond with some particular prayer or action? If so, how do you plan to respond?

_____

_____

_____

_____

18. Summarize what you have learned from the passages in this section.

_____

_____

_____

_____

_____

_____

19. List your questions about 18:35–19:44.

_____

_____

_____

_____

1. Wilcock, pages 169-170.
2. Marshall, page 710
3. E.W.G. Masterman, "Jerusalem," *The International Standard Bible Encyclopedia*, volume 3 (Grand Rapids, Mich.: William B. Eerdmans Publishing Company, 1956), page 1598.

Luke 19:45–21:4

Questions

John the Baptist was the Lord's messenger who prepared the way for the Messiah, but Herod executed him. Now, Jesus comes in the name of the Lord to His Temple (Luke 19:38,45,47; 20:1; 21:1,5,37-38) —but tragically, the Jews do "not recognize the time of God's coming" (19:44). Jesus is "the messenger of the covenant, whom you desire," but He is not what the people have in mind. Yet they do not ignore His coming; rather, they are filled with questions. Who is this? By what authority does He do the things He does? What are these claims He has made for Himself?

As you read 19:45–21:4, observe what happens when the Lord comes to His Temple, and note the questions that His coming provokes.

The cleansing (19:45-48)

The temple (19:45). See the box, "The Temple," on pages 151 and 152.

A den of robbers (19:46). The prophet Jeremiah had predicted the Babylonians would destroy the first Temple because of the people's sins. After committing all kinds of injustice, the people of Judah went unrepentant to Solomon's Temple to meet with God (Jeremiah 7:9-10), but Jeremiah said this was like treating the Temple as a refuge for robbers

143

For Thought and Discussion: a. Exactly what was Jesus denouncing in 19:45-48?

b. How was Jesus' action different from the political protests, terrorism, and violent overthrow of the government that the Zealots wanted?

c. Is Jesus' action a model for us to follow in dealing with abuses in the Church? Why, or why not? What about abuses in the secular government?

d. Jesus' action was authorized by God. How do we know this? How could the Jews have known this? How could the Zealots, Pharisees, and priests have known that their religious and political views and deeds were not authorized by God? How can we know whether our and others' actions are authorized by God or just by personal opinion?

(Jeremiah 7:11). Jesus quotes this passage of Jeremiah to denounce the Jews for being like the people of Jeremiah's day.

1. Think about Luke 19:46. In your own words, explain what Jesus found wrong with the religion being practiced at the Temple.

_____

_____

_____

_____

_____

_____

A question of authority (20:1-8)

Until Jesus entered the Temple, He clashed mainly with the unofficial "lay" leaders of Judaism—the Pharisees and experts in the Law. From the cleansing of the Temple onward, however, He confronted the official "ordained" leaders—the priests and elders. Many of these men were no friends of the Pharisees, but they recognized a common enemy in Jesus. Luke 20:1–21:38 develops the theme of 19:47-48.

The priests and elders could not arrest Jesus as a political activist because He was only behaving like a prophet and teacher (19:45-47). Yet His words and actions challenged their authority regarding Jewish doctrine and Temple management. Therefore, the leaders tried to make Jesus openly claim God's authority to teach and perform prophetic deeds (20:1-2). Perhaps then the leaders could demand proof of His claims and discredit Him before the people and Rome.

2. How did Jesus' question in 20:3-4 pose a dilemma[1] for the Jewish leaders (20:3-7)?

_____

_____

_____

_____

_____

_____

3. Why did the leaders' ability to understand Jesus'
   authority depend upon their understanding of
   John's authority (20:7-8)?

_____

_____

_____

_____

_____

The wicked tenants (20:9-19)

Now Jesus addresses a parable to the crowd in the presence of the priests and teachers. The parable recalls Isaiah 5:1-7.

Sent a servant (20:10). God sent a long series of
   prophets to Israel in Old Testament times. These
   men were often ridiculed, persecuted, and even
   killed.

Inheritance will be ours (20:14). "Jewish law provided
   that a piece of property unclaimed by an heir
   would be declared 'ownerless,' and could be
   claimed by anyone. The tenants assumed that the
   son came as heir to claim his property, and that if
   he were slain, they could claim the land."[2]

---

4. What is Jesus trying to tell the crowd in 20:9-16?

_____

_____

_____

_____

For Further Study:
Compare 20:1-8 to a
similar question of
authority in 11:14-32.
Notice how Jesus
handled such questions.
Or, compare a more
honest question in
7:18-23. Did Jesus
evidently prefer to tell
people directly what to
think of Him, or to let
them observe and draw
their own conclusions?
Can you suggest reasons
why? How did He handle
sincere and insincere
inquiries? Again, can you
think of reasons for this
preference?

**For Thought and
Discussion:** How does
the parable in 20:9-16
portray the vineyard
owner's character?

Optional Application:
Meditate on 20:18 and
its implications for your
life.

Capstone (20:17). Literally, "head of the corner." That is, either a large stone used as the lintel of a door, "a large stone used to anchor and align the corner of a wall, or the keystone of an arch."[3] Jesus quotes Psalm 118:22, part of the same Messianic psalm with which the disciples welcomed Him as King into the city only two days earlier.

Broken . . . crushed (20:18). Here Jesus combines Daniel 2:34-35 with Isaiah 8:14.

5. The crowd responds to Jesus' parable with horror (Luke 20:16). What point does Jesus make by quoting the Messianic prophecies in Luke 20:17-18?

_____

_____

_____

_____

_____

6. What does the interchange in 20:9-19 have to do with the leaders' challenge in 20:1-8?

_____

_____

_____

_____

_____

A question of taxes (20:20-26)

Taxes to Caesar (20:22). The tax in question was a poll tax to the foreign occupiers. The Jews may have carried the heaviest tax burden in the empire, for they bore the sales, customs, and poll taxes that all Roman subjects paid, on top of heavy religious dues. According to the scribes' interpretation of the Bible, Jews paid both the "first" and the "second" tithe, although modern interpreters believe that these were originally meant as alternatives (Leviticus 27:30-33, Deuteronomy 14:22-29).[4] There were also a temple tax and other dues. F.C. Grant says that *"the total taxation of the Jewish people in the time of Jesus, civil and religious combined, must have approached the intolerable proportion of between 30 and 40 percent; it may have been higher still."*[5] This total burden was the real reason for the Jews' misery,[6] but most Jews focused their fury on the Roman tribute, regarding the religious taxes as justly owed to God.

The spies thought they were posing a dilemma for Jesus. If He upheld the poll tax, the Jewish people would know He was no patriot; but if He advised the people not to pay, He could be accused of advocating revolt against Rome.

Denarius (20:24). A Roman coin worth about one day's wages. "On one side was the portrait of Emperor Tiberias and on the other the inscription in Latin: 'Tiberius Caesar Augustus, son of the divine Augustus.'"[7] Jesus drew attention to both the portrait and the inscription.

---

7. What was Jesus saying about our obligations to God and the secular government in 20:23-25?

_____

_____

_____

_____

_____

_____

For Thought and Discussion: a. Jesus implied the denarius was Caesar's because his image was on it and he'd had it made. By analogy, how can we tell what belongs to God?

b. What would it have meant in practice for the Jews to give to Caesar what was Caesar's and to God what was God's?

c. What does it mean for us to do this in practice? Think of some specific examples.

For Thought and Discussion: Did Jesus please the politically radical Zealots or the politically entrenched Sadducees by His teaching on God and Caesar? Why, or why not? How did Jesus expose the motives and priorities of both groups? What implications do these facts have for us?

A question about resurrection (20:27-40)

Sadducees (20:27). Another party within Judaism, in fierce competition with the Pharisees and the Zealots. The Sadducees were aristocratic, sympathetic with Rome, and primarily interested in

147

politics and Temple management. They controlled the high priesthood and the Sanhedrin (the counsel of elders), although some of the elders were Pharisees.[8] The Sadducees interpreted the Law of Moses literally and regarded only those five books as Scripture. They rejected the oral law of the Pharisees; they were scrupulous regarding the laws of purity and sacrifice in Leviticus; they denied the existence of angels, demons, resurrection, afterlife, and a spiritual world.[9]

8. The Sadducees quoted Scripture to Jesus: "Moses wrote . . ." (20:28); and Jesus replied with Scripture (20:37). What fault did Jesus find with the Sadducees' use of Scripture that revealed their whole religion to be misguided (20:37-38)?

_____

_____

_____

_____

Jesus' question (20:41-44)

Having silenced all His enemies, Jesus asked a question of His own.

David calls him "Lord" (20:44). Jews believed that the Messiah would descend from David (David's son) and that He would be greater than David (David's Lord). But for Jews, who believed that a man's descendants could never be greater than the man himself, these two beliefs about the Messiah seemed to conflict.

9. How was it possible that the Messiah was both David's descendant and greater than David (Romans 1:3-4)?

_____

_____

148

Optional Application:
a. Do any of the traits Jesus condemns in 20:46-47 suggest an attitude or practice you would like to resist in your own life? If so, what is it?
b. This week, plan to meditate on 20:46-47 and ask God to uproot any tendencies in you to be like this.

_____
_____
_____
_____
_____

The teachers criticized (20:45-47)

_____

Flowing robes (20:46). The teachers "wore long, white linen robes that were fringed and almost reached to the ground."[10]

Important seats (20:46). Whoever sat on the bench in front of the chest that contained the sacred scrolls could be seen by everyone else in the synagogue.[11]

Devour widows' houses (20:47). "Since the teachers of the law were not paid a regular salary, they were dependent on the generosity of patrons for their livelihood. Such a system was open to abuses, and widows were especially vulnerable to exploitation."[12]

10. Jesus condemned the teachers of the law for certain practices. What character traits did those practices show (20:46-47)?

_____
_____
_____
_____
_____

The widow's offering (21:1-4)

_____

Temple treasury (21:1). Beyond the Court of the Gentiles lay the Court of the Women. In that court were thirteen trumpet-shaped boxes for monetary offerings. Women were not permitted beyond the

149

Optional Application:
Can you think of any
way in which you could
follow the widow's
example in 21:1-4? If
so, describe how you
might do so. If not, pray
about how you might
do so.

Court of the Women, but male Jews were permitted both in that court and beyond.[13]

11. In contrast to the scribes, who profited as trustees
of widows' money (20:47), and in contrast to the
other rich people, why did Jesus praise the widow
referred to in 21:2?

_____

_____

_____

_____

_____

12. Summarize what Jesus reveals about Himself and
His opponents through His words and deeds in
19:45–21:4.

Himself_____

_____

_____

_____

_____

His opponents_____

_____

_____

_____

_____

13. Look through the optional questions in this lesson.
Then describe one way in which you could let
something in 19:45–21:4 affect your life.

_____

_____

14. List any questions you have about 19:45–21:4.

_____

_____

_____

The Temple

In order to win the good will of his Jewish subjects, Herod the Great decided to renovate the Temple in Jerusalem. The project was begun in 20 BC and not finished until AD 64, shortly before it was destroyed in the Jewish revolt. But even in AD 30, Herod's Temple was a grand complex in full operation.

With "immense sums of money,"[14] Herod had expanded the Temple to twice its former size.[15] It stood on a rock at the highest point of Jerusalem, which was itself built on a hill (Matthew 5:14). The Temple complex covered a quarter of a mile, its exterior faced with silver, gold, and "dazzling white marble."[16] From a distance, as Jesus saw it from the Mount of Olives (Luke 19:41), the Temple glittered like a snow-capped peak.

When Jesus "entered the temple area" (19:45), He came first to the outer court, called the Court of the Gentiles because Gentiles were allowed there but not inside the Temple proper. That court was crowded with people buying and selling unblemished animals for sacrifice, since pilgrims could seldom bring their own animals from long distances. There were also men who could change Greek, Roman, or other coinage into the coinage which was required for purchases and offerings in the Temple.[17]

During festival times, such as the Passover, Jerusalem's normal population of 25,000 was sometimes more than doubled by pilgrims,[18] so business was undoubtedly brisk when Jesus entered the Temple. Even though the sellers were providing a

(continued on page 152)

151

(continued from page 151)

convenient service to pilgrims, it is doubtful that they were charging fair prices for wares on which they had a monopoly. Also, there was a further problem with their presence. The Court of the Gentiles was meant to be the place where God-fearing Gentiles could worship the true God, as Jesus quoted Isaiah: "My house will be called a house of prayer for all nations" (Isaiah 56:7, Luke 19:46). All the commerce in the Court for Jewish convenience and profit was no doubt making it impossible for this ministry to foreigners to go on.[19]

In Jewish eyes, to accuse someone of violating God's will was the act of a prophet, not a political activist, even if the accusation took the form of strong action. Because Jesus acted in defense of God's Law and not against it, the Temple authorities could not arrest Him.[20] However, the Jewish Zealots probably hoped for more violent demonstrations soon.

1. Technically, a *dilemma* is a problem with exactly two alternatives, each of which has its own problems. The Pharisees were faced with two undesirable alternatives.
2. *The NIV Study Bible*, page 1518.
3. *The NIV Study Bible*, page 913.
4. Bruce, page 39.
5. F.C. Grant, *The Economic Background of the Gospels* (Oxford: Oxford University Press, 1926), 105 (his emphasis). Cited in Bruce, page 40.
6. Bruce, page 40.
7. *The NIV Study Bible*, page 1474.
8. Paul Winter, "Sadducees and Pharisees," *Jesus and His Time*, edited by Hans Jurgen Schultz, translated by Brian Watchorn (Philadelphia: Fortress Press, 1971), pages 47-50.
9. *The NIV Study Bible*, page 1476.
10. *The NIV Study Bible*, page 1520.
11. *The NIV Study Bible*, page 1520.
12. *The NIV Study Bible*, page 1520.
13. *The NIV Study Bible*, page 1520.
14. Wilcock, page 180.
15. Edouard Lohse, "Temple and Synagogue," *Jesus in His Time*, page 75.
16. Wilcock, page 180.
17. Lohse, pages 77-78.
18. Lohse, page 78.
19. Bruce, pages 189-190.
20. Bruce, page 189.

Luke 21:5–22:38

The End Approaches

When the Lord came to His Temple, He was not acknowledged; therefore, He abandoned both Temple and city to destruction (13:34-35, 19:41-44). Although Jesus spent much of the last week of His life teaching the crowds in the Temple, Luke focuses on His final lessons for the disciples. Read 21:5–22:38, observing what Jesus wanted His disciples to remember and how far short of His desires they fell.

Signs of the end (21:5-38)

Here, Jesus predicts Jerusalem's destruction in AD 70 (the beginning of the end) and also His own second coming at the end of the age. Jesus apparently means to show that the destruction of the city and Temple are separate chronologically from the coming of the Son of Man, but that both are part of the end times. The attitudes of the first Christians living through the former events and of the last Christians living through the latter events should be the same.

Not one stone (21:6). When the Romans crushed the Jewish revolt in AD 70, they leveled Jerusalem and the Temple complex. "Stones were even pried apart to collect the gold leaf that melted from the roof when the temple was set on fire."[1]

I am he (21:8). I am the Christ. This may also be a claim to be God, the I AM (Exodus 3:14).

a. Memorize 21:14-
19. Ask God to remind
you of this if you are
ever persecuted for your
faith.

b. Pray for Christians
in other countries who
are persecuted.

**For Thought and
Discussion:** People hold
many different
interpretations of "end-
times" passages. Rather
than dwelling on what
precisely is going to
happen and when, what
should we focus on in
light of the end times
(21:12-19,28,34-36)?

The end will not come right away (21:9). Luke
21:8-19 describes events that will characterize the
whole present age between Jesus' departure and
His return.[2]

1. Some of the disciples' misconceptions about the
Temple prompt Jesus to teach on the end times
(21:5-7). What are those misconceptions?

_____

_____

_____

_____

_____

2. Why is the warning Jesus gives in 21:8-9 necessary
for disciples?

_____

_____

_____

_____

3. What instructions and encouragement does Jesus
give to those who will be persecuted for proclaiming Him (21:12-19)?

_____

_____

_____

_____

_____

Not a hair . . . will perish (21:18). Luke 21:16 says
that some disciples will be put to death, but
21:18-19 promises that all who stand firm will
attain resurrection and eternal life.

Jerusalem surrounded (21:20). This sign of the end of Jerusalem was fulfilled in AD 68. The Jews had to flee to the mountains (21:21) because the city was being destroyed. Many people believe that just before Christ's second coming, Jerusalem will again be surrounded and people will again have to flee.

Times of the Gentiles (21:24). The Gentiles will "have both spiritual opportunities . . . and domination of Jerusalem" until "God's purpose for the Gentiles has been fulfilled."[3]

The Son of Man coming (21:27). Luke 21:5-6,20-24 was fulfilled in AD 70, although it may well have a second fulfillment. Luke 21:8-19 describes what is characteristic of the whole age between Jesus' two comings. Luke 21:25-28 names the signs of Jesus' second coming.

---

4. How should disciples behave in the last crisis, and why (21:28)?

_____

_____

_____

_____

_____

_____

This generation (21:32). If "generation" has its normal meaning of a life span, then Jesus probably means that His predictions will come true "in a preliminary sense in the AD 70 destruction of Jerusalem." If "generation" has its secondary meaning of "race," then Jesus means that the Jewish people will remain a distinct group until His second coming. Alternatively, Jesus may mean that the generation alive when the signs of the final end begin (21:25-28) will still be alive when He returns.[4]

For Thought and Discussion: Why do you suppose Jesus refused to give unmistakable signs of the end?

For Thought and Discussion: Do you think any of the counsel and encouragement Jesus gave in 21:5-36 is relevant today? If so, how do you think it should affect a Christian's behavior and attitudes?

For Further Study: There is a distinction between the end times we have been in since Jesus' resurrection (21:8-19) and the "end of the end" that will come when He returns (21:25-28). It is the same as the distinction between the way the Kingdom is already within and among us, and the way it is yet to come. See what else you can learn about these distinctions in the other Gospels and in the writings of Paul.

155

For Thought and Discussion: Luke says that Satan moved Judas to betray Jesus (22:3). Does that relieve Judas of responsibility for the betrayal? Why or why not? (See Matthew 27:3-5, Luke 22:22, Acts 5:1-6, 1 Peter 5:8-9).

5. How should disciples behave when turmoil seems distant (21:34-36)?

_____

_____

_____

_____

6. What most challenges or encourages you in 21:5-36? How does it affect your outlook?

_____

_____

_____

_____

Betrayal (22:1-6)

Jesus had promised that God would destroy the Temple, but Temple authorities believed that it was they who would destroy Jesus. In chapters 22 through 24, observe the plan of God and the plan of Satan coming together.

Feast . . . Passover (22:1). The Passover meal was eaten on the first evening of the Feast of Unleavened Bread, an eight-day festival in April. By New Testament times, the whole feast was often called the Passover.

The Passover commemorated the miracle by which God liberated the Israelites from Egypt (Exodus 12:1-20). God's angel of death killed every firstborn in Egypt on one night, but the angel "passed over" all who put lamb's blood on the doorframes of their houses. This plague terrified the Egyptians and moved Pharaoh to release Israel from slavery. In Luke 9:31, Luke calls the "departure" Jesus was going to fulfill in Jerusalem an *exodos*. It was not only Jesus' departure from the world, but also the liberation of all people through Jesus' blood.

The Last Supper (22:7-38)

Notice the contrast between Jesus and His disciples.

Optional Application: Meditate on the significance for you of the shared bread and cup.

The day of Unleavened Bread (22:7). The day preceding Passover evening; Thursday of Passion Week. On that day, all leaven was purged from homes and the Passover animals were killed.[5]

A man carrying a jar of water (22:10). He would have been unusual, since women carried jars but men carried leather bottles. Thus, this sign may have been prearranged.[6] Rooms were scarce in Jerusalem at Passover time, and Jesus needed a secret place for His Passover with the disciples so that He would not be arrested until the time God had chosen. Notice that even the disciples did not know where the house was, for Jesus knew there was a traitor among them.

Until it finds fulfillment (22:16). Jesus was about to fulfill the sacrifice for all time by becoming the perfect Passover Lamb (John 1:29, 1 Corinthians 5:7). When the future Kingdom is fulfilled, Jesus "will renew fellowship with those who through the ages have commemorated the Lord's Supper. Finally the fellowship will be consummated in the great Messianic 'wedding supper' to come" (Revelation 19:9).[7]

The cup (22:17,20). Four cups were shared in a traditional Passover meal; Luke tells us what Jesus said about two of them.

In remembrance of me (22:19). As the Passover recalled and proclaimed God's liberation of Israel, so the Lord's Supper would recall and proclaim God's liberation of Christians from sin and death by Christ's atoning death.

7. What meaning did Jesus give to the shared bread (22:19)?

_____

_____

_____

_____

157

Optional Application:
Churches differ on their
understanding of "This is
my body" (22:19). Ask
your pastor or another
Christian how your
church interprets this
phrase, or check several
commentaries. Luke
22:24-27 offers a
chance to practice
application within your
group. How can you
practice humility and
service among
yourselves?

New covenant (22:20). Blood was necessary to seal a
covenant (a treaty, an agreement of relationship),
whether between equals or between a lord and his
subjects (Genesis 15:8-21, Exodus 24:3-8). The
new covenant between God and man was
promised in Jerusalem (Jeremiah 31:31-34).

8. Explain the meaning of the second shared cup
(Luke 22:20).

_____

_____

_____

_____

_____

Question . . . dispute (22:23-24). While Jesus was teaching about deep spiritual matters, His disciples were
thinking on another level. First, they debated who
among them might be the traitor (22:23), and then
they turned to a second dispute (22:24). Compare
this second dispute to the argument in 9:46-48.

9. What was the disciples' dispute about (22:24)?

_____

_____

_____

_____

_____

Benefactors (22:25). Rulers like to take titles like
"Benefactor" or even "Savior" of a city or
province, even though they often did nothing to
deserve these titles.

Judging (22:30). In Israel, "judges" were leaders
(Judges 2:16). The twelve apostles were going to

become the leaders of the "twelve tribes" (the whole) of the new Israel.

10. How did behavior typical of unbelievers differ from what Jesus expected of His disciples (22:25-26)?

_____

_____

_____

_____

_____

_____

11. What reasons did Jesus give for this behavior?

22:27 _____

_____

_____

_____

_____

_____

_____

22:28-30 _____

_____

_____

_____

_____

_____

_____

For Thought and Discussion: a. Why do Christians often find it hard to act as the youngest or as servants (22:25-26)?
b. How can a Christian overcome these obstacles?

For Thought and Discussion: a. How did Peter's view of his own character differ from Jesus' knowledge of him (22:33-34)?
b. Are you ever like Peter in this way? If so, how?

For Thought and Discussion: Satan's influence over Judas raises the question of our responsibility for our actions. How can we affirm all at once that a person is responsible for allowing himself to be influenced by Satan, that Satan is responsible for influencing him, and that ultimately God is in control of each person's choices and Satan's plans? How does Jesus' betrayal show Satan's and man's plans for evil serving God's plan for good?

For Thought and Discussion: Does 22:31-38 offer any lessons for Christians today? If so, what are they?

For Thought and Discussion: a. How did the disciples misunderstand Jesus' mission (18:31-34, 22:38)?

b. Are Christians ever tempted to act as the disciples in 22:33-38? If so, in what ways?

You (22:31). Plural in Greek; Jesus is speaking of all the disciples.

12. a. What do you learn from chapter 22 about Satan's plan for . . .

Jesus (22:3-6) _____

_____

_____

_____

_____

The disciples (22:31) _____

_____

_____

_____

_____

b. How did Jesus expect the Father to use Satan's plan for His own ends (18:31-33; 22:20,32)?

_____

_____

_____

_____

13. When the disciples traveled during Jesus' life, they could count on the hospitality of those to whom they ministered (22:35). How were their needs going to be different after Jesus was executed as a criminal (22:36-37)?

_____

_____

_____

_____

That is enough (22:38). The disciples thought Jesus meant that they must arm themselves for war against Rome. They were ready to die fighting for the Messiah (22:33,38,49-51). Jesus silences them with an ironic "That's plenty!" or a curt "Enough!"

14. Did you find anything in 21:5–22:38 that you want to take to heart? If so, you can use this space to explain what seems important to you and how you might put it into practice or respond to it in prayer.

_____

_____

_____

_____

_____

15. List any questions you have about this lesson.

_____

_____

_____

_____

1. *The NIV Study Bible*, page 1477.
2. Wilcock, 187-188; *The NIV Study Bible*, page 1580.
3. *The NIV Study Bible*, page 1581.
4. *The NIV Study Bible*, page 1581; compare Marshall, pages 779-780.
5. Morris, page 304.
6. Marshall, 791-792; Morris, page 304.
7. *The NIV Study Bible*, page 1582.

Luke 22:39-23:49

Arrest, Trial, and Death

Satan's plan is moving smoothly (22:3-6). The disciples are woefully unprepared for the coming crisis (18:34; 22:23-24,31-34,38). Nevertheless, Jesus and His Father know exactly what They are doing. Read 22:39–23:49, observing how Jesus and Peter each behave in the hour of Jesus' enemies, "when darkness reigns" (22:53).

Prayer in Gethsemane (22:39-46)

The place (22:39). An olive grove called Gethsemane (Matthew 26:36), which means "oil press."[1]

Knelt down (22:41). Jews normally prayed standing,[2] but kneeling expressed Jesus' anguish, fervency, and humility.

Cup (22:42). In the Old Testament, the cup is a metaphor for God's wrathful judgment upon sin (Psalm 75:8, Isaiah 51:17, Jeremiah 25:15-28). Jesus drinks it on behalf of sinful humanity.

1. Explain Jesus' prayer in 22:42. What does it reveal about Him?

_____

_____

Optional Application:
a. Are you ever like the disciples in 22:45-46? Talk to God about this.

b. What current temptations, if any, do you need to pray about?

Optional Application:
Compare Luke 22:49-50 with Mark 14:50-52. Do you act like the disciples when your faith is challenged? What should you do?

2. What do the disciples show about themselves in this scene (22:40,45-46)?

Jesus arrested (22:47-53)

Crowd (22:47). It included Temple guards and Roman soldiers with swords, some hastily conscripted servants who carried clubs, and some of the Jewish leaders (Matthew 26:47, Mark 14:43, Luke 22:52, John 18:3).

One of them (22:50). Peter struck the blow (John 18:10).

This is your hour (22:53). Jesus has been on the road to the cross since infancy (2:34-35). He has long known His destiny; He has set His face toward it (9:51); forewarned His disciples about it (9:22, 44-45; 12:50; 17:25; 18:31-33); discussed it with Moses and Elijah (9:31); told parables about it (20:9-15); prayed about it (22:42); and determined that nothing and no one will deter Him from it (13:32-33; 22:37,51). But Jesus has also understood it and seen beyond it (18:33; 22:15-16, 19-20), for His destiny is not decreed by Satan or even blind fate, but by the loving, sovereign Father. And His Father decreed there would come a time when Jesus would be handed over to His enemies. That time has now come.

3. How do the eleven apostles react when they realize that Jesus is going to be arrested (22:49-50)?

_____

_____

_____

Optional Application: Reflect on how Jesus dealt with arrest, trial, and torture. How could you apply His example to your own situation? Ask God to enable you.

4. In light of Jesus' teaching, what does that reaction show about their characters and their understanding of Jesus? (See especially 6:27-36, 9:22-27, 22:22-38.)

_____

_____

_____

_____

_____

5. What character traits and feelings does Jesus show at His arrest (22:47-53)?

_____

_____

_____

Peter's denials (22:54-62)

Peter was the disciple with the sword (22:50). Now the Messiah whom Peter hoped would liberate Israel has gone meekly under arrest, and Peter is alone among strangers in the high priest's courtyard.

6. What happens to Peter in the courtyard after Jesus is taken inside for interrogation (22:56-62)?

_____

_____

_____

Optional Application:
Put yourself in Peter's
place in 22:54-62.
Could what happened to
Peter happen to you?
How do you know? Ask
God to strengthen you to
resist this kind of
temptation.

7. How does Peter fall short of Jesus' teaching in
12:4-12?

8. Consider Peter's reaction when he realizes he has
allowed temptation to defeat him so quickly and
completely (22:61-62). What has he learned about
himself (22:33-34)?

Before the Sanhedrin (22:63-71)

Daybreak (22:66). According to Jewish law, a trial that
could pass a death sentence could legally be held
only during daylight hours.
Luke omits two unofficial trials during the
night that the other Gospels describe: a hearing
before Annas, the high priest's father-in-law (John
18:12-24); and an unofficial trial before the Sanhedrin in the house of Caiaphas, the high priest
(Matthew 26:59-68, Mark 14:55-65).

The council of the elders (22:66). The Sanhedrin, the
high board of Jewish leaders. It included both
Pharisees and Sadducees.

9. Jesus knew that the council did not understand the titles "Christ" (22:67) and "Son of God." (22:70) the way He did. Still, how did He respond to the council's questions (22:67-70)?

For Thought and Discussion: What would you say to people who say Jesus never claimed to be the Son of God?

_____

_____

_____

_____

_____

10. How did the council interpret Jesus' response (Mark 14:63-64, Luke 22:71)?

_____

_____

_____

_____

_____

Before Pilate and Herod (23:1-25)

To Pilate (23:1). Rome did not permit the Sanhedrin "to carry out capital punishment, except in the case of a foreigner who invaded the sacred precincts of the temple."[3] Therefore, the Sanhedrin had to refer the case to the Roman governor.

Pilate had been governor of Judea since AD 26, and over the years he had made himself very unpopular with the Jews. He had provoked a riot by parading his soldiers with a portrait of the emperor on a Jewish holy day; the Jews regarded the portrait as an idol.[4] Pilate was also cruel at times (13:1), but he knew Rome would punish him if there were riots over a religious controversy.

Pilate and Herod were both conveniently in Jerusalem for the Passover, rather than in Caesarea and Tiberias, their respective headquarters.

For Thought and Discussion: Why is it important that Pilate and Herod both found Jesus innocent of breaking any law (23:13-16,22)?

11. Notice how the elders accused Jesus to the Roman governor (23:2). Were their charges just? How do you know (Luke 20:20-26, 22:49-52; John 18:36)?

_____

_____

_____

_____

_____

It is as you say (23:3). Luke omits the details of Pilate's interrogation (compare John 18:33-38), recording only one question. Jesus' reply is literally, "The statement is yours."[5] This is an idiomatic Jewish way of saying yes; it also implies that Pilate is speaking the truth but does not know what "king of the Jews" means.

12. Why did Pilate pronounce Jesus innocent (23:4, 13-15)? How did Pilate interpret the elders' accusation and Jesus' words (23:1-4)?

_____

_____

_____

_____

_____

Sent him to Herod (23:7). This might have let Pilate evade responsibility for a delicate political case. It was also a diplomatic gesture toward an enemy whose good will Pilate needed. Pilate and Herod had been quarreling over jurisdiction, but Herod was pleased when Pilate referred a case to him (23:12).

Barabbas (23:18). The name means "son of Abba" or "son of the father." It is ironic that Jesus died in place of a man with this name. Barabbas was plainly a dangerous criminal, probably a Zealot terrorist (23:19). It was customary for the governor to release one prisoner at Passover (Mark 15:6-8).

13. Describe Herod's attitude toward Jesus (23:8-11).

_____

_____

_____

_____

_____

Crucifixion (23:26-43)

Seized Simon (23:26). A victim normally carried his own cross, but Jesus must have been too weak from His beatings to carry a thirty- to forty-pound beam.[6]

Weep for yourselves (23:28). Jesus foresaw the suffering Jerusalem would endure when Rome besieged the city.

14. How does 23:28-31 suggest Jesus felt toward His mourners?

_____

_____

_____

_____

_____

15. Describe Jesus' attitude toward His executioners (23:34).

_____

_____

For Further Study: Did Pilate condemn Jesus for wrongdoing or for some other reason? How can you tell (23:20-25)?

For Thought and Discussion: How is Jesus' conduct in 22:39–23:25 a model for Christians? Name some specific ways.

Optional Application: Think about how the account of Jesus' arrest, abandonment, and trial makes you regard Jesus and yourself. Are you moved to respond in any way? If so, how?

For Further Study: Paraphrase 23:31. Who or what do you think were the green tree and the dry? What were "these things" that were being done? You may want to look up references to "green tree" in the Old Testament, such as Jeremiah 11:16-17 and 17:7-8.

For Further Study:
Describe the second
criminal's attitude
toward Jesus
(23:40-42). What did he
apparently believe
about:
■ justice?
■ mercy?
■ salvation?
■ Jesus' identity?

Both criminals (23:32). Crucifixion was reserved for the basest criminals and slaves. Roman citizens were not crucified, for people regarded this form of execution as an unspeakable disgrace.

The Skull (23:33). The Latin word *Calvaria* gives us the name "Calvary."

16. The rulers, soldiers, and first criminal talk about the Christ and salvation several times in 23:35-39. What does their scoffing imply they believe about . . .

What it means to be the Christ? _____

_____

_____

_____

_____

What salvation means? _____

_____

_____

_____

_____

17. What do Jesus' responses to the second criminal (23:43) and to the sneering crowd tell you about Him?

_____

_____

_____

_____

_____

_____

Death (23:44-49)

The sixth hour . . . ninth hour (23:44). Noon to three p.m.

The curtain of the temple (23:45). It separated the Holy Place, where priests entered daily to offer prayers, from the Holy of Holies, where only the high priest entered once a year to offer sacrifice for the sins of the people. Hebrews 9:1-15 and 10:19-22 explains the significance of the tearing of the curtain: Christ's death permanently opened the way to God's presence.

Into your hands (23:46). The Septuagint version of Psalm 31:5 was used in Jewish evening prayer before sleep. Jesus quoted it in Luke 23:46.[7]

---

18. Describe the attitude with which Jesus met death (23:46).

_____

_____

_____

_____

This was a righteous man (23:47). "Or, 'this man was the Righteous One.' Matthew and Mark report the centurion's words as 'this man was the Son (or son) of God.' 'The Righteous One' and 'the Son of God' would have been essentially equivalent terms. Likewise 'the son of God' and 'a righteous man' would have been virtual equivalents." We don't know whether the centurion was confessing faith in Jesus' divinity, but he was at least testifying that Jesus was innocent.[8]

171

Optional Application:
Meditate on Jesus'
attitude toward mockers
and persecutors.
Specifically, how could
you follow His example
in your daily life? Ask
Him to enable you to do
this.

Optional Application:
Meditate on the
significance for you of:
■ the darkening sun
■ the tearing of the
  Temple curtain
■ Jesus' attitude in
  death

Optional Application:
Consider how Peter, the
other disciples, Pilate,
Herod, and the crowd
treated Jesus in
22:39–23:35. Do any of
their actions suggest an
attitude you need to
guard against? If so,
what steps might you
take toward preventing
yourself from having
similar attitudes?

Optional Application:
Meditate on how you are
like Barabbas and how
Jesus has done for you
what He did for that
criminal (23:25). Does
this resemblance lead
you to any response?

Your response

19. What does 22:39–23:49 contribute to the unfolding
    of the good news?

    _____

    _____

    _____

    _____

20. a. What one insight about Jesus' or other people's
       actions would you like to let influence your life?

    _____

    _____

    _____

    b. How can you go about taking this to heart and
       acting on it?

    _____

    _____

    _____

    _____

21. List any questions you have about this lesson.

    _____

    _____

    _____

1. *The NIV Study Bible*, page 1523.
2. Marshall, page 830.
3. *The NIV Study Bible*, page 1486.
4. J.I. Packer, Merrill C. Tenney, and William White, Jr., *The World of the New Testament* (Nashville, Tenn.: Thomas Nelson Publishers, 1982), page 82.
5. Marshall, page 853.
6. *The NIV Study Bible*, page 1528.
7. Marshall, pages 875-876.
8. *The NIV Study Bible*, page 1587.

Luke 23:50–24:53

Resurrection and Ascension

Jesus has been arrested, tried, convicted, sentenced and executed. His disciples have scattered and the women who followed Him are just about the only ones left to watch Him take His last breath (23:49). And yet, what everyone thought was a huge victory for Satan turns out to be his biggest defeat—and a resounding triumph for the Son of God! As you read Luke 23:50–24:53, note especially the tremendous reversals that God brings about.

Burial (23:50-56)

A member of the Council (23:50). Joseph was apparently absent when the Sanhedrin convicted Jesus, for Mark 14:64 says "all" supported the decision to condemn Jesus.

It required extraordinary courage for a council member to request Jesus' body. Criminals often were left unburied as paupers, and normally only family members were permitted to take their bodies. Joseph was proclaiming his disagreement with the Sanhedrin's decision. John adds that Nicodemus accompanied Joseph when he made his request for the body (John 19:39).

Preparation Day (23:54). Friday was called this because people had to prepare for the Sabbath, which began at sunset on Friday. For instance, food could not be cooked on the Sabbath.

173

For Thought and Discussion: What does the Resurrection prove (Romans 1:4)?

Optional Application: What difference does Jesus' resurrection make to your life and the way you respond to your circumstances?

1. How does 23:50-56 fulfill Isaiah's prophecy in Isaiah 53:9? What is significant about this?

_____

_____

_____

_____

_____

_____

Resurrection (24:1-12)

Two men (24:4). Angels in human form. Matthew and Mark mention only one of them, the spokesman (Matthew 28:2, Mark 16:5), and they record additional words of this conversation.[1]

2. What did the women find when they went to Jesus' tomb at dawn on Sunday (24:2-8)?

_____

_____

_____

_____

_____

3. What did the "men" say to the women at the tomb (24:5-7)?

_____

_____

_____

_____

_____

4. How did the apostles respond to the women's report (24:9-12)?

_____

_____

_____

_____

For Thought and Discussion: Is 24:30,35 meant to remind us of 22:19? If so, what significance does this have for us?

The walk to Emmaus (24:13-35)

When Jesus encounters the two disciples on the road to Emmaus, they are discussing the events of the past week with sorrow and confusion (24:14,17).

5. Observe why the two disciples are sad and confused.

   a. How do they describe their former Master, whom they used to call the Christ (24:19)?

   _____

   _____

   _____

   _____

   _____

   b. What disappointing and confusing things have happened (24:20-24)?

   _____

   _____

   _____

   _____

   _____

175

6. Why does Jesus call His disciples "foolish" and "slow of heart" (24:25)? Compare 24:19-24 with 24:26.

_____

_____

_____

_____

Moses and all the prophets (24:27). A name for the entire Old Testament.

---

7. How does Jesus relieve the disciples' sorrow and confusion (24:27,30-32)?

_____

_____

_____

_____

8. Think about how we are in the same position as these two disciples. What lessons for our lives can we learn from their encounter with Jesus on the road?

_____

_____

_____

_____

_____

9. What happened in Jerusalem while the two disciples were gone (24:34)?

_____

_____

_____

_____

_____

_____

The appearance to the disciples (24:36-49)

_____

Jesus himself stood among them (24:36). Jesus' resurrected body was different from a natural body, so
He could enter a locked room (Mark 16:12, John
20:19).

_____

10. a. At least three of those present already had seen
Jesus risen, and everyone else had believed them
(24:33-35). Still, how did everyone react when
Jesus suddenly appeared (24:37)?

_____

_____

_____

_____

b. Why do you think they reacted in this way?

_____

_____

_____

_____

_____

11. How did Jesus prove He had a physical body
(24:38-43)?

_____

_____

_____

_____

Optional Application:
a. Ask Jesus to reveal
Himself to you and
enable you to
understand the events of
His life.
b. Decide to find out
what the Old Testament
says about Jesus
(24:27).

177

Optional Application:
How does 24:45-48
apply to us today? How
could you act on these
instructions more fully?

Law . . . Psalms (24:44). The whole Old Testament. Jesus spoke not just of specific prophecies, but also of the whole Scripture's message about man's sin and need for salvation, and God's just and merciful unfolding of a plan of salvation that led toward the Messiah.

12. What two sets of events did Jesus say the Old Testament had prophesied?

    24:46 _____

    _____

    _____

    24:47 _____

    _____

    _____

13. What part did the disciples have in fulfilling this prophecy, and why (24:47-48)?

    _____

    _____

    _____

    _____

    _____

14. Luke 12:12 and Acts 1:4-5 explain "what my Father has promised" (Luke 24:49). When would the disciples begin their ministry?

    _____

    _____

    _____

    _____

    _____

The Ascension (24:50-53)

In his Gospel, Luke telescopes the time of these last events so that it seems as though Jesus ascended on Easter Sunday. Luke's book of Acts, however, makes it clear that Jesus ascended forty days later (Acts 1:3,9).

15. How did the disciples respond to their new understanding of Jesus (24:52-53)?

_____

_____

_____

_____

_____

Temple (24:53). Luke's Gospel ends where it begins. Zechariah prayed in the Temple for Israel's deliverance, and the disciples return there praising God for answering that prayer. Yet God would soon destroy Herod's Temple and reveal that His true temple is the community of believers (1 Corinthians 3:16, Ephesians 2:19-22, 1 Peter 2:4-5).

16. Why was it necessary for Jesus to die?

_____

_____

_____

_____

17. Why was it necessary for Jesus to rise again?

_____

_____

_____

18. What do these events mean to you, personally?
    How have you responded to them? Explain.

    _____

    _____

    _____

    _____

    _____

19. Is there anything in this lesson that you would like
    to respond to? What is it? What would you like to
    do about it?

    _____

    _____

    _____

    _____

    _____

20. List any questions you have about 23:50–24:53.

    _____

    _____

    _____

    _____

    _____

1. *The NIV Study Bible*, page 1587.

Looking Back

By now you should have a thorough grasp of Luke's
Gospel and could even explain Jesus' life and teaching
to anyone curious about the Christian faith. Right? On
the other hand, perhaps you have forgotten a great deal
of what you studied in early lessons. We have tried to
help you tie the book together as you went along, but a
review is the best way to clarify and reinforce what you
have learned.

If you can, reread or skim the whole Gospel of
Luke and glance through the past fifteen lessons. If this
sounds like more time than you can afford, a half-hour
of reviewing the previous lessons, rereading the outline
(on pages 15-17), and thumbing through Luke's
Gospel should probably bring back to you the most
important things you've learned. Recall from lesson
one what you thought the book's main messages were.

As you review the Gospel, jot answers to questions
1-6. Some relevant verses are suggested for each question, but don't feel that you must look at all of these or
only these. Also, don't treat the questions like a comprehensive, final exam that requires deep theologizing.
Instead, imagine yourself explaining these things to a
nonChristian inquirer. Your goal here is to be able to
explain the gospel to ordinary people.

1. What does it mean that Jesus is *the Christ?* See
   1:32-33,78-79; 2:11,32; 3:22,38; 4:18-21; 9:20-22;
   20:41-44; 21:25-28; 22:19-22; 23:3,33; 24:26.

For Further Study:
Review Jesus' teaching
on one of the following
topics:
- Judgment
- Repentance
- Women
- Children
- The poor and
  disreputable
- Wealth
- The Holy Spirit
- Prayer
- Faith
- The Sabbath
- The Law
- Healing

2. What does Luke's Gospel tell us about *salvation*?
What does it mean to be saved? How are people
saved in this Gospel? What does God or Jesus do?
What does the person do? See 1:47-55,68-79;
2:29-32; 4:18-19,40-41; 5:14,20,31-32; 7:47-50;
8:48; 10:25-28; 15:1-32; 17:17-19; 18:13-14,18-30;
19:1-10; 23:42-43.

3. According to Luke, for whom is the *gospel* (good
news) intended? See 1:54; 2:32; 4:18; 6:20-22;
7:37; 8:43; 15:1-2; 18:16; 19:2; 23:40-44.

4. What is *the Kingdom of God*? See 1:32-33; 2:14;
4:18-19; 6:20-22; 7:22; 10:9; 11:20; 12:31-34;
13:18-21,24-30; 14:12-24; 15:22-24; 17:20-25;
22:16,29-30.

_____

_____

_____

5. How would you describe Jesus' *character* as Luke portrays Him?

_____

_____

_____

_____

_____

6. What have you learned about what a *disciple* is and does? See 5:10; 6:22,27-49; 8:15,21,24-25; 9:1-5,13,23-26,48,57-62; 10:1-12,16-24,39; 11:1-13; 12:11-12,22-48; 14:7-35; 16:8-13; 17:1-10; 18:1-8,28-30; 19:12-26; 21:12-19; 22:19,25-30; 24:45-49,52-53.

_____

_____

_____

_____

_____

7. Briefly explain the most *important points of the gospel* as you understand it from Luke. If you use terms like *Christ, Son of God,* or *saved,* be sure you know what they mean. See 4:18-21; 24:19-26,46-48.

_____

_____

_____

_____

_____

_____

_____

8. Have you noticed any areas (thoughts, attitudes, opinions, behavior) in which you have changed as a result of your study of Luke's Gospel? If so, describe them.

_____

_____

_____

_____

_____

_____

9. Look back over the entire study at questions in which you expressed a desire to make some specific personal application. Are you satisfied with your follow-through? Why, or why not? Pray about any of those areas that you think you should continue to pursue. (Now that you have completed this study, perhaps something new has come to mind that you would like to concentrate on. If so, bring it before God in prayer.)

Write anything you decide below.

_____

_____

_____

_____

_____

_____

Summary

One way of dealing with a major review is to get a large pad of paper or a markerboard. Beginning with question 1, ask the group to brainstorm everything they remember about the meaning of the title *Christ*. List the group's thoughts. After about five minutes of brainstorming, ask the group to summarize the list into a sentence or two of clear, concise definition—something everyone can remember and explain to nonChristians. Then continue to brainstorm and summarize question 2, and so on.

Be sure to save at least ten to fifteen minutes to examine how you've changed (question 8) and how you plan to continue applying what you've learned (question 9). This is a time to encourage and motivate each other to keep going. You may not see dramatic changes in your lives yet; instead, you may see areas you want to continue praying and acting on. Remind the group that God is responsible for results; we are responsible for consistent prayer and trust.

If anyone still has questions about Luke, plan ways of finding answers. The sources beginning on page 187 may help.

Finally, evaluate how well your group functioned during your study of Luke. Some questions you might ask:

- What did you learn about small group study?
- How well did your study help you to grasp the book of Luke?
- What were the most important truths you discovered together about God?
- What did you like best about your meetings?
- What did you like least? What would you change?
- How well did you meet the goals you set at the beginning?
- What are members' current needs? What will you do next?

Now thank God for what He has taught you about Himself and you. Thank Him for specific ways He is changing you through your study of Luke's Gospel. Thank Him also for your group, and for the freedom to study the Bible together.

Study Aids

For further information on the material covered in this study, consider the following sources. If your local bookstore does not have them, you can ask the bookstore to order them from the publishers, or find them in a public, university, or seminary library.

Commentaries on Luke

Geldenhuys, Norval. *The Gospel of Luke* (New International Commentary on the New Testament, Eerdmans, 1951).
   Scholarly; readable for laymen; less thorough than Marshall, but also less expensive and lengthy. Offers the insight of Dutch scholars not often noted by English writers.

Hendriksen, William. *Luke* (New Testament Commentary, Baker, 1978).
   An expository, or sermon-like, approach to verse-by-verse commentary. Very readable and inspiring. Separates analysis of the Greek from the main exposition to avoid troubling the layman. Each section includes "Practical Lessons"—suggestions of how the passage applies today.

Liefeld, Walter L. *Luke* (The Expositor's Bible Commentary, ed. Frank E. Gaebelein, Zondervan, 1984).
   A part of one of the best series of expository commentaries to come out in recent times. Includes comments on Greek occasionally in the main text, but these are never obtrusive and usually add to the point under review. More technical discussions are saved for the notes.

Marshall, I. Howard. *The Gospel of Luke* (New International Greek Testament Commentary, Eerdmans, 1978).
   The most thorough and up-to-date commentary on Luke's Gospel now available. Exceptionally readable, despite its length and the number of

references. Ignorance of Greek should not hinder anyone willing to tackle a long book, but this book is especially useful if you are just researching a particular passage.

Morris, Leon. *The Gospel According to Saint Luke* (Tyndale New Testament Commentary, Eerdmans, 1974).
Concise and well-researched, and available in an inexpensive paperback edition. An ordinary person can read straight through this one for good background, cross-references, and comments. Morris omits most of the critical discussions of sources, parallels in the other Gospels, etc., that Marshall and Geldenhuys address.

Wilcock, Michael. *Savior of the World* (The Bible Speaks Today Series, InterVarsity, 1979).
Not a verse-by-verse analysis like the above, but instead exposition of each passage with excellent application to the present day. Wilcock is especially good at fitting a particular passage into the train of thought of the chapter and the themes of the whole book. The scholarship is kept in the background. This is an inexpensive paperback.

Historical sources

Bruce, F.F. *New Testament History* (Doubleday, 1971).
A readable history of Herodian kings, Roman governors, philosophical schools, Jewish sects, Jesus, the early Jerusalem church, Paul, and early gentile Christianity. Well-documented with footnotes for the serious student, but the notes do not intrude.

Edersheim, Alfred. *The Life and Times of Jesus the Messiah* (Eerdmans, 1971).
Reprint of the classic two-volume original (second edition) of 1886. Some of the material is out-of-date, but most is still sound. The prose of this life of Jesus is of timeless value. Edersheim was a converted Jew, and his knowledge of the Jewish law makes this book outstanding.

Harrison, E.F. *Introduction to the New Testament* (Eerdmans, 1971).
History from Alexander the Great—who made Greek culture dominant in the biblical world—through philosophies, pagan and Jewish religion, Jesus' ministry and teaching, and the spread of Christianity. Very good maps and photographs of the land, art, and architecture of New Testament times.

Concordances, dictionaries, and handbooks

A *concordance* lists words of the Bible alphabetically along with each verse in which the word appears. It lets you do your own word studies. An *exhaustive* concordance lists every word used in a given translation, while an *abridged* or *complete* concordance omits either some words, some occurrences of the word, or both.

Two of the three best exhaustive concordances are the venerable *Strong's Exhaustive Concordance* and *Young's Analytical Concordance to the Bible*. Both are available based on the King James Version of the Bible and the New American Standard Bible. *Strong's* has an index by which you can find out which Greek or Hebrew word is used in a given English verse (although its information is occasionally outdated). *Young's* breaks up each English word it translates. Neither concordance requires knowledge of the original languages.

Perhaps the best exhaustive concordance currently on the market is *The NIV Exhaustive Concordance*. It features a Hebrew-to-English and a Greek-to-English lexicon (based on the eclectic text underlying the NIV), which are also keyed to Strong's numbering system.

Among other good, less expensive concordances, *Cruden's Complete Concordance* is keyed to the King James and Revised Versions, *The NIV Complete Concordance* is keyed to the New International Version. These include all references to every word included, but they omit "minor" words. They also lack indexes to the original languages.

A **Bible dictionary** or **Bible encyclopedia** alphabetically lists articles about people, places, doctrines, important words, customs, and geography of the Bible.

The New Bible Dictionary, edited by J.D. Douglas, F.F. Bruce, J.I. Packer, N. Hillyer, D. Guthrie, A.R. Millard, and D.J. Wiseman (Tyndale, 1982) is more comprehensive than most dictionaries. Its 1300 pages include quantities of information along with excellent maps, charts, diagrams, and an index for cross-referencing.

Unger's Bible Dictionary by Merrill F. Unger (Moody, 1979) is equally good and is available in an inexpensive paperback edition.

The Zondervan Pictorial Encyclopedia edited by Merrill C. Tenney (Zondervan, 1975, 1976) is excellent and exhaustive, and was revised and updated in the '80s. Its five 1000-page volumes represent a real financial investment, however, and all but very serious students may prefer to use it at a church, public, college, or seminary library.

Unlike a Bible dictionary in the above sense, *Vine's Expository Dictionary of New Testament Words* by W.E. Vine (various publishers) alphabetically lists major words used in the King James Version and defines each New Testament Greek word that KJV translates with that English word. *Vine's* lists verse references where that Greek word appears, so that you can do your own cross-references and word studies without knowing any Greek.

Vine's is a good, basic book for beginners, but it is much less complete than other Greek helps for English speakers. More serious students might prefer *The New International Dictionary of New Testament Theology,* edited by Colin Brown (Zondervan) or *The Theological Dictionary of the New Testament* by Gerhard Kittel and Gerhard Friedrich, abridged in one volume by Geoffrey W. Bromiley (Eerdmans).

A **Bible atlas** can be a great aid to understanding what is going on in a book of the Bible and how geography affected events. Here are a few good choices.

The MacMillan Atlas by Yohanan Aharoni and Michael Avi-Yonah (MacMillan, 1968, 1977) contains 264 maps, 89 photos, and 12 graphics. The many maps of individual events portray battles, movements of people, and changes of boundaries in detail.

The New Bible Atlas by J.J. Bimson and J.P. Kane (Tyndale, 1985) has 73 maps, 34 photos, and 34 graphics. Its evangelical perspective, concise and helpful text, and excellent research make it a very good choice, but its greatest strength is its outstanding graphics, such as cross-sections of the Dead Sea.

The Bible Mapbook by Simon Jenkins (Lion, 1984) is much shorter and less expensive than most other atlases, so it offers a good first taste of the usefulness of maps. It contains 91 simple maps, very little text, and 20 graphics. Some of the graphics are computer-generated and intriguing.

The Moody Atlas of Bible Lands by Barry J. Beitzel (Moody, 1984), is scholarly, very evangelical, and full of theological text, indexes, and references. This admirable reference work will be too deep and costly for some, but Beitzel shows vividly how God prepared the land of Israel perfectly for the acts of salvation He was going to accomplish in it.

A ***handbook*** of biblical customs can also be useful. Some good ones are *Today's Handbook of Bible Times and Customs* by William L. Coleman (Bethany, 1984) and the less detailed *Daily Life in Bible Times* (Nelson, 1982).

For small group leaders

Getting Together: A Guide for Good Groups by Em Griffin (InterVarsity, 1982).
Applies to all kinds of groups, not just Bible studies. From his own experience, Griffin draws deep insights into why people join groups; how people relate to each other; and principles of leadership, decision-making, and discussions. It is fun to read, but its 229 pages will take more time than the above books.

How to Build a Small Groups Ministry by Neal F. McBride (NavPress, 1994).
This hands-on workbook for pastors and lay leaders includes everything you need to know to develop a plan that fits your unique church. Through basic principles, case studies, and worksheets, McBride leads you through twelve logical steps for organizing and administering a small groups ministry.

How to Lead Small Groups by Neal F. McBride (NavPress, 1990).
Covers leadership skills for all kinds of small groups—Bible study, fellowship, task, and support groups. Filled with step-by-step guidance and practical exercises to help you grasp the critical aspects of small group leadership and dynamics.

The Small Group Leader's Handbook by Steve Barker, et. al. (InterVarsity, 1982)
Written by an InterVarsity small group with college students primarily in mind. It includes more than the above book on small group dynamics and how to lead in light of them, and many ideas for worship, building community, and outreach. It has a good chapter on doing inductive Bible study.

You Can Start a Bible Study Group by Gladys Hunt (Harold Shaw, 1984).
Builds on Hunt's thirty years of experience leading groups. This book is wonderfully focused on God's enabling. It is both clear and applicable for Bible study groups of all kinds.

DJ Plus, a special section in *Discipleship Journal* (NavPress, bimonthly).

Unique. Three pages of this feature are packed with practical ideas for small groups. Writers discuss what they are currently doing as small group members and leaders. To subscribe, write to Subscription Services, Post Office Box 54470, Boulder, Colorado 80323-4470.

Bible study methods

Braga, James. *How to Study the Bible* (Multnomah, 1982).

Clear chapters on a variety of approaches to Bible study: synthetic, geographical, cultural, historical, doctrinal, practical, and so on. Designed to help the ordinary person without seminary training to use these approaches.

Fee, Gordon, and Douglas Stuart. *How to Read the Bible for All Its Worth* (Zondervan, 1982).

After explaining in general what interpretation and application are, Fee and Stuart offer chapters on interpreting and applying the different kinds of writing in the Bible: Epistles, Gospels, Old Testament Law, Old Testament narrative, the Prophets, Psalms, Wisdom, and Revelation. Fee and Stuart also suggest good commentaries on each biblical book. They write as evangelical scholars who personally recognize Scripture as God's Word for their daily lives.

Jensen, Irving L. *Independent Bible Study* (Moody, 1963), and *Enjoy Your Bible* (Moody, 1962).

The former is a comprehensive introduction to the inductive Bible study method, especially the use of synthetic charts. The latter is a simpler introduction to the subject.

Wald, Oletta. *The Joy of Discovery in Bible Study* (Augsburg, 1975).

Wald focuses on issues such as how to observe all that is in a text, how to ask questions of a text, how to use grammar and passage structure to see the writer's point, and so on. Very helpful on these subjects.